THE DIVINITY OF JESUS

IN THE BOOK OF JEREMIAH

Dr. Maxwell Shimba

Shimba Publishing, LLC.

Printed by Shimba Publishing LLC
Printed in the United States of America

TABLE OF CONTENTS

INTRODUCTION

The divinity of Jesus Christ is one of the cornerstones of Christian faith and doctrine. This belief rests on the conviction that Jesus is not only the Messiah but also the incarnate God, fulfilling the promises of the Old Testament. While the Hebrew Scriptures primarily focus on God's covenant with Israel, Christians maintain that the Old Testament anticipates the coming of a divine Redeemer. The Book of Jeremiah, one of the major prophetic books of the Old Testament, offers important foreshadowings of the Messiah's divine nature. By analyzing key passages in Jeremiah, we can uncover how they connect to the life, ministry, and divinity of Jesus Christ.

The idea of divine foreshadowing in the Old Testament is essential in understanding the relationship between the Old and New Covenants. Jesus Himself alluded to this in passages such as John 5:39, where He said, "You search the Scriptures because you think that in them you have eternal life; and it is they that bear witness about me" (ESV).

Christians believe that these "Scriptures" include prophecies and types from the Old Testament that point toward Jesus. Jeremiah, as one of the preeminent prophetic books, contains several such key references. When interpreted in the light of the New Testament, these passages offer a deeper understanding of Jesus' divinity and role as the fulfillment of God's plan for redemption.

Jeremiah's Historical and Prophetic Role

Before delving into the prophetic words of Jeremiah concerning the Messiah, it is crucial to understand the historical and theological context in which Jeremiah ministered. Jeremiah's mission occurred during one of the darkest periods of Israel's history, as the Southern Kingdom of Judah faced destruction due to its disobedience to God. Jeremiah prophesied from around 627 B.C. to 586 B.C., warning the people of impending judgment from Babylon while also offering hope of eventual restoration.

Jeremiah's prophecies often highlight the failures of the leadership in Judah—kings, priests, and false prophets who led the people astray (Jeremiah 23:1-2). Yet amidst these rebukes, he also speaks of a future time of deliverance. It is within these prophetic promises of restoration that Christians find glimpses of the coming Messiah. Specifically, Jeremiah 23:5-6 speaks of a "Righteous Branch" who would be a king from David's line:

> "Behold, the days are coming, declares the LORD, when I will raise up for David a righteous Branch, and he shall reign as king and deal wisely, and shall execute justice and righteousness in the land. In his days Judah will be saved, and Israel will dwell securely. And this is the name by which he will be called: 'The LORD is our righteousness.'" (ESV)

This "Righteous Branch" is a key messianic prophecy that points to the coming of a divine king. The phrase, "The LORD is our righteousness" (in Hebrew, YHWH Tsidkenu), refers not to just any human ruler but someone who embodies divine attributes. This prophecy has been traditionally interpreted by Christians as pointing directly to Jesus Christ, who is not only a descendant of David but also the incarnate God, as confirmed in the New Testament in passages like Romans 1:3-4, where Paul identifies Jesus as "descended from David according to the flesh and was declared to be the Son of God in power."

Exploring Key Themes in Jeremiah Through Christological Lenses

One of the essential tasks in exploring the divinity of Jesus in the Book of Jeremiah is to identify the recurring themes of judgment, justice, restoration, and the new covenant. These elements are central to the prophetic message of Jeremiah and are reflected in the New Testament revelation of Jesus Christ. By utilizing tools such as Strong's Concordance and comprehensive commentaries, we can explore these themes with greater depth.

The New Covenant in Jeremiah, for example, is perhaps one of the clearest anticipations of Jesus' divine mission and fulfillment of God's promises. In Jeremiah 31:31-34, the prophet speaks of a coming new covenant:

> "Behold, the days are coming, declares the LORD, when I will make a new covenant with the house of Israel and the house of Judah... For this is the covenant that I will make with the house of Israel after those days, declares the LORD: I will put my law within them, and I will write it on their hearts. And I will be their God, and they shall be my people." (ESV)

This promise of a new covenant, written on the hearts of the people, is explicitly linked to Jesus in the New Testament. The author of Hebrews draws a direct connection between Jesus and the new covenant prophesied in Jeremiah. In Hebrews 8:6-13, the writer quotes Jeremiah extensively, underscoring the belief that Jesus' sacrificial death instituted this new covenant, which was internal and transformative in nature, unlike the old covenant that was external and ceremonial.

Strong's Concordance provides additional insight into this passage by offering the Hebrew meanings of key terms like "law" (Torah) and "heart" (leb), emphasizing that this new covenant involves an internal, spiritual transformation rather than mere legalistic observance. In Christian theology, this transformation is made possible through the indwelling of the Holy Spirit, given by Jesus as a sign of the new covenant.

Messianic Prophecies and the Divine King

Throughout Jeremiah, there are further glimpses of a messianic figure who will fulfill the divine promises. Jeremiah 30:9 states that God will raise up "David their king," which Christians interpret as a reference to the coming Messiah. This is significant when viewed in light of New Testament declarations, such as in John 1:49, where Nathanael confesses Jesus as the "Son of God" and "King of Israel." The royal and divine nature of Jesus is echoed through the Scriptures, affirming His place not just as a king, but as the King of Kings.

Jeremiah's vision of God as the "everlasting King" in Jeremiah 10:10 also prefigures Christ's eternal kingship, as seen in Revelation 11:15, where it is proclaimed that "The kingdom of the world has become the kingdom of our Lord and of his Christ, and he shall reign forever and ever."

Strong's Concordance further enhances our understanding of terms such as "everlasting" (olam), showing that this reign is without end, eternal in nature—qualities that only God can possess. This aligns with Christian beliefs about the nature of Jesus as eternally divine.

The Divinity of the Righteous Branch

As discussed earlier, the "Righteous Branch" is one of the most explicit messianic prophecies in the book of Jeremiah. The use of the divine name YHWH in the title "The LORD is our righteousness" is pivotal. According to Strong's Concordance, the Hebrew word for righteousness, tsidkenu, carries connotations of justice, vindication, and moral uprightness—qualities that are fully realized in Christ, as attested in 2 Corinthians 5:21, where Paul declares that "God made him who had no sin to be sin for us, so that in him we might become the righteousness of God."

Christians believe that Jesus embodies this divine righteousness. His ability to provide salvation to all who believe (Romans 10:9-10) rests on His unique nature as both God and man. The prophecies in Jeremiah about the Righteous Branch are thus seen as direct indicators of Jesus' divine role in human salvation.

The Book of Jeremiah, though written centuries before the birth of Christ, contains key prophetic passages that Christians believe point to the coming Messiah—Jesus. These passages, when interpreted through the lens of the New Testament, reveal the divinity of Jesus Christ as the Righteous Branch, the King of Israel, and the mediator of a New

Covenant. Through tools such as Strong's Concordance and comprehensive commentaries, one can explore the depth of these passages, uncovering the layers of meaning that anticipate the divine mission of Christ.

In sum, the Book of Jeremiah serves as a foundational text that bridges the Old Testament prophecies with the New Testament revelation of Jesus as the incarnate God. This theological connection not only strengthens the Christian understanding of the continuity of Scripture but also affirms the divinity of Jesus Christ as foretold by the prophet Jeremiah.

DR. MAXWELL SHIMBA

CHAPTER 01

THE HISTORICAL CONTEXT OF JEREMIAH

The Book of Jeremiah was written during one of the most turbulent and pivotal periods in the history of Israel, specifically focusing on the Kingdom of Judah. Jeremiah, often referred to as the "weeping prophet" because of his deep sorrow over the spiritual state of his people, served as a prophet during the final decades of Judah's independence. His ministry spanned from approximately 627 B.C. until after the fall of Jerusalem in 586 B.C. His prophetic messages covered a range of themes including imminent judgment, the people's disobedience, and hope for future restoration.

Jeremiah's prophecies are steeped in the historical and political turmoil of his time, and they provide not only a record of Judah's fall but also contain deeper theological meanings that resonate with Christian interpretations of the coming Messiah. By understanding the historical setting of

Jeremiah, we can better grasp the context of his prophecies and the significance they hold in Christian theology.

1.1 The Political and Social Climate of Judah

Jeremiah began his ministry during the reign of King Josiah, a time of reform and renewal in Judah. Josiah was a righteous king who sought to restore the worship of Yahweh by tearing down idols and centralizing worship in Jerusalem, as recorded in 2 Kings 22-23. However, despite Josiah's efforts, the hearts of the people remained hardened. After his death, the subsequent kings of Judah—Jehoahaz, Jehoiakim, Jehoiachin, and Zedekiah—were all unfaithful to God, leading the nation further into moral and spiritual decline.

Judah faced external threats from powerful empires during this period, primarily from Babylon. Under King Nebuchadnezzar, Babylon emerged as a dominant force, conquering Assyria and expanding its empire into the Near East. Judah became a vassal state of Babylon, but rebellion against Babylonian rule—prompted by political alliances with Egypt—ultimately led to the siege and destruction of Jerusalem in 586 B.C. The Babylonian exile, a key event in Jewish history, marked the beginning of the seventy years of captivity prophesied by Jeremiah (Jeremiah 25:11).

Jeremiah's prophecies during this period were marked by a strong message of judgment. He warned that Judah's disobedience and refusal to repent would lead to devastation. He was often at odds with other prophets and political leaders who preached a message of false hope, assuring the people that God would protect them from Babylon without requiring their repentance.

1.2 The Spiritual Condition of Judah

While the political situation was dire, Jeremiah's primary concern was the spiritual condition of the people. The Book of Jeremiah is filled with God's lament over the people's idolatry, social injustice, and disregard for His covenant. In Jeremiah 2:13, God declares:

> "My people have committed two evils: they have forsaken me, the fountain of living waters, and hewed out cisterns for themselves, broken cisterns that can hold no water" (ESV).

This metaphor of forsaking the "fountain of living waters" reflects the spiritual adultery of Judah. The people had turned away from their covenant relationship with Yahweh and were worshipping false gods. Jeremiah frequently condemned their participation in pagan practices, including child sacrifice to the god Molech (Jeremiah 7:31), which led to the moral and spiritual decay of the nation.

Jeremiah's role as a prophet was to call the people back to faithfulness. However, his message of repentance was often rejected, leading him to feel isolated and persecuted. In Jeremiah 20:7-9, he expresses his deep anguish:

> "O LORD, you have deceived me, and I was deceived; you are stronger than I, and you have prevailed. I have become a laughingstock all the day; everyone mocks me. For whenever I speak, I cry out, I shout, 'Violence and destruction!' For the word of the LORD has become for me a reproach and derision all day long. If I say, 'I will not mention him, or speak any more in his name,' there is in my heart as it were a burning fire shut up in my bones, and I am weary with holding it in, and I cannot" (ESV).

Despite his suffering, Jeremiah continued to deliver God's message faithfully, foretelling not only the destruction of Jerusalem but also the future restoration of Israel. His words, therefore, contain both judgment and hope—two essential themes in the theology of Jeremiah.

1.3 Themes of Judgment and Restoration

One of the dominant themes of Jeremiah's ministry is the dual message of judgment and restoration. God's covenant with Israel, first established through Moses at Sinai, contained blessings for obedience and curses for disobedience (Deuteronomy 28). The people's failure to live up to this covenant resulted in God's judgment, which Jeremiah proclaimed with unwavering conviction. He compared the people's rebellion to spiritual adultery, repeatedly calling them to repentance.

Jeremiah's prophetic role emphasized the holiness of God, who could not tolerate sin indefinitely. In Jeremiah 5:1-3, the prophet laments:

> "Run to and fro through the streets of Jerusalem, look and take note! Search her squares to see if you can find a man, one who does justice and seeks truth, that I may pardon her. Though they say, 'As the LORD lives,' yet they swear falsely. O LORD, do not your eyes look for truth? You have struck them down, but they felt no anguish; you have consumed them, but they refused to take correction" (ESV).

This highlights the depth of the people's corruption and their refusal to heed God's discipline. However, amid these dire warnings, Jeremiah also speaks of a future hope. In Jeremiah 29:10-14, God promises that after seventy years of exile, He will bring His people back from captivity:

> "For thus says the LORD: When seventy years are completed for Babylon, I will visit you, and I will fulfill to you my promise and bring you back to this place. For I know the plans I have for you, declares the LORD, plans for welfare and not for evil, to give you a future and a hope. Then you will call upon me and come and pray to me, and I will hear

you. You will seek me and find me, when you seek me with all your heart" (ESV).

This prophecy of restoration reflects God's faithfulness to His covenant, even after His people's rebellion. The promise of a future return from exile was not only a message of hope for the people of Judah but also, from a Christian perspective, a foreshadowing of the ultimate restoration through the coming Messiah.

1.4 The Shadow of the Messiah

Jeremiah's prophecies often allude to a future hope beyond the immediate return from Babylonian exile. Christians believe these passages point forward to the coming of Jesus Christ, the Messiah who would bring about spiritual and eternal restoration. The most direct messianic prophecy in Jeremiah is found in Jeremiah 23:5-6, where the prophet speaks of a "Righteous Branch" from the line of David:

> "Behold, the days are coming, declares the LORD, when I will raise up for David a righteous Branch, and he shall reign as king and deal wisely, and shall execute justice and righteousness in the land. In his days Judah will be saved, and Israel will dwell securely. And this is the name by which he will be called: 'The LORD is our righteousness'" (ESV).

The phrase "The LORD is our righteousness" (YHWH Tsidkenu) is especially significant in understanding this passage from a Christian perspective. It points to the divine nature of this future king, who will embody God's righteousness and provide salvation not only for Israel but for all humanity. Christians interpret this as a prophecy of Jesus Christ, who is both fully divine and fully human, fulfilling the role of the righteous king and savior.

In addition to the Righteous Branch, Jeremiah's prophecy of the New Covenant in Jeremiah 31:31-34 is another key passage pointing to the Messiah:

> "Behold, the days are coming, declares the LORD, when I will make a new covenant with the house of Israel and the house of Judah... For this is the covenant that I will make with the house of Israel after those days, declares the LORD: I will put my law within them, and I will write it on their hearts. And I will be their God, and they shall be my people" (ESV).

The New Covenant, which Christians believe was established through the life, death, and resurrection of Jesus, is marked by an internal transformation—God's law written on the hearts of His people through the Holy Spirit. This spiritual renewal, prophesied by Jeremiah, is central to Christian soteriology, the doctrine of salvation.

The historical context of Jeremiah provides essential background for understanding the prophetic messages contained within the book. Jeremiah's ministry took place during a time of national crisis, as Judah faced the looming threat of Babylon and the consequences of its disobedience to God. His prophecies were filled with themes of judgment, reflecting God's holiness and justice, but also with messages of restoration and hope for the future.

For Christians, Jeremiah's prophecies take on an additional layer of meaning. The prophet's declarations about a coming Righteous Branch, the New Covenant, and the restoration of Israel are seen as foreshadowings of the coming Messiah—Jesus Christ. By studying the historical and spiritual context of Jeremiah's time, we can better appreciate the depth of his prophecies and their fulfillment in the person and work of Jesus. Through this lens, Jeremiah's words speak not only to ancient Judah but also to all who seek salvation through the divine righteousness of Christ.

Judah's Decline

Judah's Political, Social, and Religious State during Jeremiah's Time

The Book of Jeremiah unfolds during one of the most turbulent periods in the history of ancient Israel, specifically focusing on the Kingdom of Judah. The decline of Judah in the late 7th and early 6th centuries B.C. was marked by a series of internal and external crises that ultimately led to the nation's destruction at the hands of the Babylonian Empire. The political instability, social corruption, and religious apostasy of this period form the backdrop of Jeremiah's prophetic ministry. This chapter will provide a detailed review of these conditions, offering a deeper understanding of why Judah faced divine judgment and how these events paved the way for the hope of messianic restoration that Jeremiah prophesied.

1.1 The Political State of Judah

During the time of Jeremiah, Judah was experiencing significant political instability. Following the reign of King Josiah, Judah entered a period of rapid decline due to weak leadership, external threats, and shifting alliances. Josiah, one of the last righteous kings of Judah, had initiated religious reforms, reinstituted the proper worship of Yahweh and attempted to rid the land of idolatry. However, after his death in 609 B.C., the political landscape of Judah quickly deteriorated.

The Kings After Josiah:

- Jehoahaz (Shallum), Josiah's son, briefly reigned for three months before being deposed by Pharaoh Neco of Egypt. Egypt then placed Jehoiakim, another of Josiah's sons, on the throne as a puppet king (2 Kings 23:31-34). This marked the beginning of Judah's vassal status to foreign powers, as it became a pawn in the larger geopolitical struggles between Egypt and Babylon.

- Jehoiakim, who reigned from 609-598 B.C., was a wicked and corrupt king. He rebelled against Babylonian control, despite being installed by Egypt. His rebellion resulted in the first of Babylon's military campaigns against Judah, and in 598 B.C., Nebuchadnezzar laid siege to Jerusalem. Jehoiakim died during this siege, and his son Jehoiachin ascended to the throne.

- Jehoiachin (also called Jeconiah or Coniah), like his father, ruled during a time of crisis. He reigned for only three months before surrendering to Nebuchadnezzar, who exiled him to Babylon in 597 B.C. along with many of Judah's elite and craftsmen.

- Zedekiah, the last king of Judah, was appointed by Nebuchadnezzar but later rebelled against Babylon. This rebellion led to the second and final siege of Jerusalem in 586 B.C., resulting in the city's destruction and the beginning of the Babylonian exile. Zedekiah was captured, blinded, and taken to Babylon, marking the end of the Davidic monarchy for that period (2 Kings 24-25).

This period of political turmoil, marked by weak leadership and poor decisions, directly contributed to Judah's downfall. The kings of Judah, after Josiah, failed to heed the warnings of the prophets, especially Jeremiah, and instead relied on ill-fated alliances with Egypt and other nations. Jeremiah repeatedly warned against trusting in these foreign powers, calling the people to trust in Yahweh alone (Jeremiah 2:18), but his advice was ignored.

Jeremiah 21:8-9 provides a summary of the stark political reality of Judah at that time:

> "And to this people you shall say: 'Thus says the LORD: Behold, I set before you the way of life and the way of death. He who stays in this city shall die by the sword, by famine, and by pestilence, but he who goes out and surrenders to the Chaldeans who are besieging you shall live and shall have his life as a prize of war.'" (ESV)

1.2 The Social Corruption of Judah

Judah's political decline was mirrored by deep social corruption. Jeremiah's prophecies often reveal the extent to which the social fabric of Judah had unraveled. The people, especially the leaders, had become morally bankrupt. Corruption was rampant among the political, religious, and social elites, and the nation was characterized by greed, oppression of the poor, and a lack of justice.

Social Injustice and Exploitation

Jeremiah's writings frequently highlight the social injustices perpetrated by the leaders of Judah. The wealthy and powerful were exploiting the poor and perverting justice. The prophet declares in Jeremiah 5:26-28:

> "For wicked men are found among my people; they lurk like fowlers lying in wait. They set a trap; they catch men. Like a cage full of birds, their houses are full of deceit; therefore they have become great and rich; they have grown fat and sleek. They know no bounds in deeds of evil; they judge not with justice the cause of the fatherless, to make it prosper, and they do not defend the rights of the needy" (ESV).

This passage illustrates the systemic injustice that had become endemic in Judah. The leadership, instead of protecting the vulnerable, were enriching themselves at the expense of the poor and marginalized. Widows, orphans, and the poor were often left without justice, a direct violation of the Mosaic Law, which commanded that these groups be treated with fairness and compassion (Deuteronomy 24:17-22).

The Hardness of Heart

Not only were the people engaged in overt acts of injustice, but their hearts had become calloused and indifferent to the warnings of God. Jeremiah compares their spiritual condition to hardened stone, stating in Jeremiah 5:3:

> "O LORD, do not your eyes look for truth? You have struck them down, but they felt no anguish; you have consumed them, but they refused to take correction. They have made their faces harder than rock; they have refused to repent" (ESV).

The lack of repentance, even in the face of God's discipline, is a recurring theme in Jeremiah. Despite suffering consequences such as famine, war, and pestilence, the people of Judah continued in their stubborn ways. Their refusal to repent not only led to social corruption but also exacerbated their political vulnerability.

1.3 Religious Apostasy in Judah

One of the most significant causes of Judah's decline, according to Jeremiah, was the nation's spiritual rebellion against God. Despite being chosen as God's covenant people, Judah had turned away from the worship of Yahweh and had embraced idolatry and pagan religious practices. Jeremiah's prophecies are filled with condemnations of this religious apostasy.

The Worship of False Gods

Judah's religious decline can be traced to its adoption of the religious practices of surrounding nations. The people worshiped Baal, Asherah, and other Canaanite deities, even going so far as to sacrifice their children in the fire to Molech. Jeremiah laments in Jeremiah 19:4-5:

> "Because the people have forsaken me and have profaned this place by making offerings in it to other gods whom neither they nor their fathers nor the kings of Judah have known; and because they have filled this place with the blood of innocents, and have built the high places of Baal to burn their sons in the fire as burnt offerings to Baal, which I did not command or decree, nor did it come into my mind…" (ESV).

The depth of Judah's idolatry is further illustrated by their construction of altars to these false gods in the temple of Yahweh itself, an egregious violation of the covenant God made with Israel.

False Prophets and Deceptive Leadership

In addition to the rampant idolatry, the religious leadership in Judah was corrupt. False prophets arose, leading the people astray with comforting lies, assuring them of peace when in reality, disaster was imminent. Jeremiah rebukes these false prophets in Jeremiah 14:13-14:

> "Then I said: 'Ah, Lord GOD, behold, the prophets say to them, "You shall not see the sword, nor shall you have famine, but I will give you assured peace in this place."' And the LORD said to me: 'The prophets are prophesying lies in

my name. I did not send them, nor did I command them or speak to them. They are prophesying to you a lying vision, worthless divination, and the deceit of their own minds.'" (ESV).

These false prophets contributed to the spiritual decline of Judah by giving the people a false sense of security, convincing them that God's judgment would not come. Jeremiah, however, faithfully proclaimed the true word of the LORD, even as he was mocked, imprisoned, and persecuted for his messages of warning and repentance.

1.4 Theological Significance of Judah's Decline

The political, social, and religious decline of Judah was not merely a result of poor leadership or external pressures—it was, according to Jeremiah, the result of the people's unfaithfulness to God. Judah's failure to uphold the covenant they made with Yahweh at Sinai led to their downfall. This covenant, which established Israel as God's chosen people, demanded exclusive worship of Yahweh and obedience to His laws. The people's violation of these requirements—especially their idolatry—brought about divine judgment.

In Jeremiah 2:11-13, God expresses His amazement at Judah's unfaithfulness:

> "Has a nation changed its gods, even though they are no gods? But my people have changed their glory for that

which does not profit. Be appalled, O heavens, at this; be shocked, be utterly desolate, declares the LORD, for my people have committed two evils: they have forsaken me, the fountain of living waters, and hewed out cisterns for themselves, broken cisterns that can hold no water" (ESV).

This passage illustrates the theological depth of Judah's apostasy. They had not only abandoned God, the source of life and sustenance, but they had replaced Him with worthless idols that could not satisfy or save. Jeremiah's message is clear: the political, social, and religious collapse of Judah was the direct result of their spiritual adultery and failure to honor God's covenant.

Judah's decline during the time of Jeremiah was a multifaceted crisis involving political instability, social injustice, and religious apostasy. The nation, once blessed under the righteous reign of kings like David and Josiah, had fallen into a state of corruption and rebellion against God. Jeremiah's prophetic ministry was a response to this national crisis, as he called the people to repentance and warned of the impending judgment.

At the same time, Jeremiah's prophecies also pointed to a future hope—a time when God would restore His people and establish a new covenant. In this context, many Christians see in Jeremiah's words a foreshadowing of the coming

Messiah, who would ultimately bring about the true restoration and salvation of not only Judah but the entire world.

Jeremiah's Mission: A Call to Repentance and Hope

1. Introduction to Jeremiah's Prophetic Mission

Jeremiah's prophetic mission was one of the most challenging and emotionally fraught in the history of Israel's prophets. Tasked with delivering God's messages to the people of Judah during the final years of its existence as an independent kingdom, Jeremiah's words carried the weight of impending doom. His mission spanned more than four decades, from roughly 627 B.C. until after the fall of Jerusalem in 586 B.C. During this time, he prophesied under multiple kings, facing relentless opposition from political, religious, and social leaders who rejected his messages.

At the heart of Jeremiah's mission was a call to repentance. The nation of Judah had strayed far from its covenantal relationship with God, indulging in idolatry, social injustice, and false worship. Jeremiah was sent to warn the people of the catastrophic consequences of their rebellion. Yet, his message was not solely one of judgment. Alongside his warnings of destruction were prophecies of future hope— hope for restoration, renewal, and a new covenant that would bind God and His people in a transformative relationship.

Jeremiah's mission, therefore, can be understood in two key dimensions: the call to repentance and the promise of hope and restoration.

2. The Call to Repentance

Throughout his ministry, Jeremiah consistently called the people of Judah to turn back to God and abandon their sinful ways. His prophecies reveal the depth of Judah's spiritual decay, as the nation had forsaken Yahweh and turned to idols, corrupt practices, and false prophets. Jeremiah's role was to awaken the people to the impending consequences of their actions—judgment in the form of destruction and exile—while urging them to seek God's mercy through genuine repentance.

2.1 Judah's Idolatry and Apostasy

One of the primary concerns of Jeremiah's prophetic mission was addressing the pervasive idolatry that had taken hold of Judah. The people had forsaken their covenant relationship with God and had embraced the worship of false gods, particularly Baal, Asherah, and Molech. These practices often involved heinous rituals, including child sacrifice, which Jeremiah condemned in the strongest terms. In Jeremiah 7:9-10, God, through the prophet, lists the people's sins:

> "Will you steal, murder, commit adultery, swear falsely, make offerings to Baal, and go after other gods that

you have not known, and then come and stand before me in this house, which is called by my name, and say, 'We are delivered!'—only to go on doing all these abominations?" (ESV)

This passage encapsulates the hypocrisy of the people. They believed that because they had the Temple in Jerusalem, God would continue to protect them, regardless of their sins. Jeremiah warned them that their idolatry and apostasy would lead to the destruction of the Temple and the city itself unless they repented.

2.2 The Broken Covenant

Jeremiah's mission was also centered on the theme of covenant. God had made a covenant with Israel at Mount Sinai, binding the people to exclusive worship of Yahweh and adherence to His laws. By the time of Jeremiah's ministry, Judah had repeatedly violated this covenant, provoking God's judgment. In Jeremiah 11:10, God describes the severity of Judah's breach:

> "They have turned back to the iniquities of their forefathers, who refused to hear my words. They have gone after other gods to serve them. The house of Israel and the house of Judah have broken my covenant that I made with their fathers." (ESV)

Jeremiah repeatedly called the people to return to God and renew their covenantal relationship. The word shuv, meaning "to turn" or "to repent," is central to Jeremiah's message, as he urged the people to turn back from their sinful ways and realign themselves with God's will. Jeremiah 3:12 expresses this plea for repentance:

> "Return, faithless Israel, declares the LORD. I will not look on you in anger, for I am merciful, declares the LORD; I will not be angry forever." (ESV)

God's desire for His people to repent is evident in Jeremiah's prophecies. Even as judgment loomed, God extended the opportunity for mercy and forgiveness, if only the people would turn from their idolatry and injustice.

2.3 Rejection of False Prophets and Leaders

Another key element of Jeremiah's mission was his confrontation with false prophets and corrupt leaders who misled the people. These false prophets proclaimed that peace and safety were assured, even as Babylon's armies approached. Jeremiah, however, delivered the opposite message: Judah's destruction was imminent unless the nation repented. In Jeremiah 6:13-14, God condemns the false prophets for their deceit:

> "For from the least to the greatest of them, everyone is greedy for unjust gain; and from prophet to priest,

everyone deals falsely. They have healed the wound of my people lightly, saying, 'Peace, peace,' when there is no peace." (ESV)

Jeremiah's mission was made more difficult by the fact that these false prophets had the ear of the people and the support of Judah's leaders. In contrast, Jeremiah's messages of impending judgment were unpopular and often met with resistance. His life was frequently in danger, as his prophecies challenged the complacency of the people and the corruption of those in power.

3. The Promise of Hope and Restoration

Though Jeremiah's ministry is often remembered for its focus on judgment and destruction, it also carried a profound message of hope. God, through Jeremiah, did not leave His people without the promise of restoration. This promise was not only for Judah's physical return from exile but also for a deeper spiritual renewal that would come in the form of a new covenant.

3.1 Hope Beyond Exile

One of the central aspects of Jeremiah's message of hope is the assurance that the exile to Babylon would not be the end for Judah. While judgment was inevitable, God promised that after a period of seventy years, He would bring

His people back to their land. In Jeremiah 29:10-14, God reassures the exiles:

> "For thus says the LORD: When seventy years are completed for Babylon, I will visit you, and I will fulfill to you my promise and bring you back to this place. For I know the plans I have for you, declares the LORD, plans for welfare and not for evil, to give you a future and a hope." (ESV)

This promise of restoration gave the people hope during their time in exile, reminding them that God had not abandoned them. Even in their punishment, God's ultimate plan was one of redemption and renewal. The return from exile would serve as a foreshadowing of the deeper spiritual restoration that Jeremiah also foretold.

3.2 The New Covenant

Perhaps the most significant aspect of Jeremiah's prophetic mission concerning hope is the promise of a New Covenant. This covenant would differ from the Mosaic covenant, which was external, based on written laws that the people repeatedly failed to keep. Instead, the New Covenant would be internal, written on the hearts of the people, and would bring about a deeper, more transformative relationship between God and His people. In Jeremiah 31:31-34, God declares:

> "Behold, the days are coming, declares the LORD, when I will make a new covenant with the house of Israel and the house of Judah… For this is the covenant that I will make with the house of Israel after those days, declares the LORD: I will put my law within them, and I will write it on their hearts. And I will be their God, and they shall be my people… For I will forgive their iniquity, and I will remember their sin no more." (ESV)

This promise of the New Covenant is central to Christian theology, as it points forward to the coming of Jesus Christ, who Christians believe established this covenant through His death and resurrection. The New Covenant would be based on grace, internal transformation, and forgiveness, rather than on the strict legal adherence required by the old covenant.

3.3 The Righteous Branch

In addition to the New Covenant, Jeremiah also prophesied the coming of a righteous ruler from the line of David, who would bring salvation and justice to God's people. This messianic prophecy is found in Jeremiah 23:5-6:

> "Behold, the days are coming, declares the LORD, when I will raise up for David a righteous Branch, and he shall reign as king and deal wisely, and shall execute justice and righteousness in the land. In his days Judah will be saved, and

Israel will dwell securely. And this is the name by which he will be called: 'The LORD is our righteousness.'" (ESV)

Christians interpret this prophecy as a direct reference to Jesus Christ, the Messiah, who would come to fulfill the promises made to David's house and bring ultimate salvation not only to Israel but to the entire world. The title "The LORD is our righteousness" (YHWH Tsidkenu) reflects the divine nature of this coming king, emphasizing that He would embody God's righteousness.

4. Conclusion: Jeremiah's Dual Mission

Jeremiah's prophetic mission was both a warning of impending judgment and a message of hope for future restoration. He was called to confront Judah's rampant idolatry, social injustice, and covenant unfaithfulness, urging the people to repent before it was too late. However, Jeremiah's mission also included the promise that God had not abandoned His people, even in the face of exile

Through the prophecies of the New Covenant and the Righteous Branch, Jeremiah pointed toward a future in which God would restore His people, not just physically but spiritually as well.

For Christians, Jeremiah's mission holds profound significance. His prophecies of a New Covenant and a righteous king find their ultimate fulfillment in Jesus Christ, who Christians believe came to establish a new relationship between God and humanity. Thus, while Jeremiah is often remembered as the "weeping prophet" of doom and destruction, his mission also contained the seeds of hope and salvation.

CHAPTER 02

THE BRANCH OF RIGHTEOUNESS

One of the most profound and significant messianic prophecies in the Book of Jeremiah is found in Jeremiah 23:5-6, where the prophet speaks of the "Branch of Righteousness." This passage offers a glimpse into the future hope for the people of Israel and Judah—one rooted in God's promise of a righteous king from the line of David. Christians view this prophecy as a direct reference to Jesus Christ, the long-awaited Messiah who would fulfill the roles of both a divine ruler and savior.

The prophecy reads:

> "Behold, the days are coming," declares the LORD, "When I will raise up for David a righteous Branch, and He

will reign as king and act wisely and do justice and righteousness in the land. In His days Judah will be saved, and Israel will dwell securely; and this is His name by which He will be called, 'The LORD our righteousness'" (ESV).

This passage holds immense theological importance in both Jewish and Christian traditions, but the Christian interpretation places a special emphasis on Jesus as the fulfillment of the prophecy. In this chapter, we will explore the implications of the "Branch of Righteousness" and how it has been understood as a prophetic vision of the coming Messiah—Jesus.

2.1 The Context of the Branch of Righteousness

The prophecy of the "Branch of Righteousness" emerges in the broader context of Judah's decline, the corruption of its leaders, and the people's need for hope. At this point in Jeremiah's ministry, Judah was ruled by a series of wicked kings, most notably Jehoiakim and Zedekiah, who had led the nation into idolatry, injustice, and rebellion against God. Jeremiah had delivered harsh warnings of the coming judgment, which would ultimately result in the destruction of Jerusalem and the Babylonian exile.

Against this backdrop of judgment and despair, Jeremiah offers a message of hope—a righteous king who would come from the line of David to restore justice and righteousness. The promise of the "Branch" provided assurance that despite the failings of human kings, God's covenant with David would not be broken. God had made a covenant with David in 2 Samuel 7:12-16, promising that David's lineage would continue forever and that one of his descendants would establish an eternal kingdom. Jeremiah's prophecy reaffirms this covenant, even as Judah faced destruction.

Jeremiah's use of the word Branch (tsemach in Hebrew) is significant. In ancient Israel, a "branch" or "shoot" was often used as a metaphor for new life emerging from what appeared to be a dead or decayed situation. In this case, the "Branch" represents new hope springing forth from the failing Davidic dynasty. Despite the unfaithfulness of Judah's leaders, God would remain faithful to His promise and raise up a righteous king—a new Davidic ruler who would embody divine wisdom and justice.

2.2 The Character of the Righteous Branch

Jeremiah's prophecy describes the coming ruler as a "righteous Branch" who would reign with wisdom and justice. These attributes stand in direct contrast to the corrupt kings of Jeremiah's day, who were characterized by selfishness, injustice, and idolatry.

- Righteousness: The Hebrew word for "righteous" (tsaddiq) carries connotations of moral integrity, justice, and a right relationship with God. The "righteous Branch" would not merely adhere to human standards of righteousness but would embody the divine standard of justice and holiness. This concept of righteousness is central to the messianic hope in the Bible. For Christians, Jesus is the ultimate fulfillment of this righteousness, as seen in the New Testament, where He is described as "the Righteous One" (Acts 7:52) and the one "who knew no sin" but became sin for humanity's sake, so that "in Him we might become the righteousness of God" (2 Corinthians 5:21).

- Wisdom: The prophecy highlights that this king would "act wisely." In contrast to the foolish and rebellious kings of Judah, the Branch of Righteousness would rule with divine wisdom. In Christian theology, Jesus is often identified as the embodiment of divine wisdom. 1 Corinthians 1:30 refers to Jesus as "our wisdom from God," linking Him to the wisdom literature of the Old Testament, where wisdom is associated with God's creative and redemptive power.

- Justice and Peace: The future king would "do justice and righteousness in the land" and provide security for Judah and Israel. This portrayal aligns with the messianic hope expressed in other parts of the Old Testament, where the

Messiah is described as one who will bring about true justice and peace. Isaiah 9:6-7 speaks of the Messiah as the "Prince of Peace" who will reign on David's throne "with justice and righteousness from that time on and forever."

This description of the Branch not only points to His moral and ethical character but also sets Him apart as a king whose reign will result in salvation and security for God's people.

2.3 The Divine Nature of the Branch: "The LORD Our Righteousness"

The final and most significant aspect of the prophecy is the name by which the Branch will be called: "The LORD is our righteousness" (YHWH Tsidkenu). This title has profound theological implications, as it connects the king directly with God's own identity.

In the Bible, names are not merely labels but are deeply tied to the identity and nature of a person. The name YHWH Tsidkenu suggests that the coming king would embody the very righteousness of God. This title is unique in its direct application of the divine name YHWH (the Tetragrammaton, the sacred name of God) to the Messiah. It indicates that the king would not only rule with divine righteousness but would also provide righteousness for the people.

In Christian theology, this phrase is seen as a direct reference to the divinity of Jesus. Jesus is not only seen as a righteous king but as the one through whom humanity is made righteous. Romans 3:22 speaks of "the righteousness of God through faith in Jesus Christ for all who believe." Jesus fulfills the role of the one who imparts righteousness to believers, making them right with God through His atoning sacrifice.

Philippians 3:9 further elaborates on this theme, with Paul declaring that his righteousness comes "through faith in Christ, the righteousness from God that depends on faith." This understanding of Jesus as "the LORD our righteousness" is central to Christian soteriology, the doctrine of salvation. Jesus' life, death, and resurrection provide the means through which humanity is justified—declared righteous in the sight of God.

2.4 The Role of the Righteous Branch in Salvation and Security

Jeremiah's prophecy also emphasizes the role of the Righteous Branch in bringing about salvation and security for Judah and Israel:

> "In His days Judah will be saved, and Israel will dwell securely" (Jeremiah 23:6, ESV).

This promise of salvation is central to messianic hope. For the people of Judah, who faced destruction and exile, the idea of salvation was both physical and spiritual. They longed for deliverance from their enemies and for the restoration of their land. However, Christians interpret this promise in a broader, spiritual sense, seeing in it a reference to the salvation brought by Jesus.

The New Testament frequently describes Jesus as the Savior who delivers His people from sin and death. Matthew 1:21 declares that Jesus "will save His people from their sins," and Luke 2:11 announces His birth as "a Savior, who is Christ the Lord." The salvation offered by Jesus extends beyond the immediate political and military concerns of Judah and encompasses the eternal spiritual needs of humanity.

Similarly, the promise of security finds its ultimate fulfillment in the peace that Jesus brings. In the Gospel of John, Jesus promises His followers a peace that transcends worldly understanding: "Peace I leave with you; my peace I give to you. Not as the world gives do I give to you" (John 14:27). This peace is not merely the absence of conflict but the profound assurance of safety and wholeness that comes from being in right relationship with God.

2.5 The Branch of Righteousness in the Broader Messianic Tradition

The prophecy of the Branch of Righteousness in Jeremiah is not an isolated passage but is part of a broader biblical tradition that speaks of a future Davidic ruler who will bring about justice, righteousness, and peace. Other prophets, including Isaiah and Zechariah, also use the imagery of a branch or shoot to describe the coming Messiah.

- Isaiah 11:1-2: "There shall come forth a shoot from the stump of Jesse, and a branch from his roots shall bear fruit. And the Spirit of the LORD shall rest upon him, the Spirit of wisdom and understanding, the Spirit of counsel and might, the Spirit of knowledge and the fear of the LORD."

- Zechariah 3:8: "Behold, I will bring my servant the Branch."

These prophecies collectively point to a future king who will fulfill God's promises to David and establish an eternal kingdom characterized by justice, peace, and righteousness.

In Christian theology, these prophecies converge in the person of Jesus Christ. He is seen as the fulfillment of the Davidic covenant, the one who embodies divine wisdom and righteousness, and the one who will reign eternally as King of Kings and Lord of Lords.

Conclusion: The Fulfillment of the Branch of Righteousness in Jesus

Jeremiah's

prophecy of the "Branch of Righteousness" is a profound messianic promise that finds its ultimate fulfillment in Jesus Christ. As the righteous king from the line of David, Jesus embodies the wisdom, justice, and righteousness foretold by the prophets. His divine title, "The LORD our righteousness," points to His unique role as both God and Savior, the one through whom humanity is made righteous.

For Christians, this prophecy holds deep theological significance. It not only affirms Jesus' identity as the Messiah but also underscores the transformative nature of His salvation. Through His life, death, and resurrection, Jesus offers righteousness to all who believe in Him, fulfilling the ancient promise of a king who would reign with justice and bring salvation and peace to His people.

Thus, the "Branch of Righteousness" stands as a beacon of hope in Jeremiah's prophecies—a hope that reaches its fullest expression in the person and work of Jesus Christ, the righteous King and divine Savior.

Messianic Expectation

1. Introduction to the Messianic Expectation

The concept of a Messiah—an anointed leader who would restore Israel to its former glory—was deeply embedded in Jewish thought during the centuries leading up to the birth of Jesus. Rooted in the promises made by God to David and further developed by the prophets, Jewish messianic expectations revolved around the coming of a Davidic king who would deliver Israel from oppression, establish justice, and reign in righteousness.

Throughout the Hebrew Scriptures, especially in the writings of the prophets like Jeremiah, Isaiah, and Ezekiel, this expectation grew into a hope that one day, a descendant of David would restore not only the political fortunes of Israel but also its spiritual fidelity to God.

For Christians, these messianic expectations find their ultimate fulfillment in Jesus Christ. Christians believe that Jesus is the promised Messiah, the one who fulfills the hopes and prophecies of the Old Testament regarding the Davidic king. This chapter will explore the Jewish messianic expectation of a Davidic ruler and how this aligns with the Christian belief in Jesus as the ultimate fulfillment of these hopes.

2. The Jewish Expectation of a Davidic King

2.1 The Davidic Covenant and the Promise of a Perpetual Kingdom

The foundation of Jewish messianic expectations is rooted in the covenant God made with David in 2 Samuel

7:12-16. This passage is often referred to as the Davidic Covenant, in which God promises David an eternal dynasty:

> "When your days are fulfilled and you lie down with your fathers, I will raise up your offspring after you, who shall come from your body, and I will establish his kingdom. He shall build a house for my name, and I will establish the throne of his kingdom forever. I will be to him a father, and he shall be to me a son... And your house and your kingdom shall be made sure forever before me. Your throne shall be established forever." (ESV)

This promise forms the bedrock of Jewish hopes for a future Davidic king, one who would reign with justice, righteousness, and eternal peace. The immediate fulfillment of this promise was seen in David's son Solomon, who succeeded him as king and built the temple in Jerusalem. However, as Solomon's reign ended in disobedience and subsequent generations of Davidic kings failed to live up to God's standards, the Jewish people looked beyond the immediate monarchy to a future time when a greater king from David's line would arise.

2.2 Prophetic Development of the Messianic Expectation

Over time, the concept of a future Davidic king was further developed by the prophets, who elaborated on the character and mission of the coming Messiah. During times of national crisis—especially during the Assyrian and Babylonian exiles—the hope for a Davidic ruler took on even greater significance.

- Isaiah's Vision of the Davidic Messiah: The prophet Isaiah, writing in the 8th century B.C., provided one of the most famous messianic prophecies, describing a future ruler who would come from the "stump of Jesse" (David's father). In Isaiah 11:1-5, we read:

> "There shall come forth a shoot from the stump of Jesse, and a branch from his roots shall bear fruit. And the Spirit of the LORD shall rest upon him, the Spirit of wisdom and understanding, the Spirit of counsel and might, the Spirit of knowledge and the fear of the LORD. And his delight shall be in the fear of the LORD. He shall not judge by what his eyes see, or decide disputes by what his ears hear, but with righteousness he shall judge the poor, and decide with equity for the meek of the earth; and he shall strike the earth with the rod of his mouth, and with the breath of his lips he shall kill the wicked. Righteousness shall be the belt of his waist, and faithfulness the belt of his loins." (ESV)

This vision of the Davidic king emphasizes the righteous rule of the Messiah, characterized by wisdom, justice, and a deep connection to God. This passage, along with others in Isaiah (such as Isaiah 9:6-7), became central to Jewish messianic expectations.

- Jeremiah's Promise of a Righteous Branch: In Jeremiah 23:5-6, the prophet expands on the promise of a future king from David's line who would reign with wisdom and righteousness. This passage, which speaks of the "Branch of Righteousness," echoes the hopes of Isaiah and other prophets for a divinely anointed ruler who would deliver Israel from oppression and restore the nation's fortunes.

- Ezekiel's Shepherd-King: Ezekiel, another major prophet writing during the Babylonian exile, also contributed to the messianic expectation. In Ezekiel 34:23-24, the prophet speaks of God raising up a shepherd from the line of David to lead His people: "And I will set up over them one shepherd, my servant David, and he shall feed them: he shall feed them and be their shepherd. And I, the LORD, will be their God, and my servant David shall be prince among them." (ESV)

While Ezekiel uses the name "David," this is understood as a reference to a future Davidic king who would be a "shepherd" to God's people. This shepherd imagery is significant, as it later becomes associated with Jesus, who identifies Himself as the "Good Shepherd" in John 10:11.

3. Messianic Hope in the Second Temple Period

During the Second Temple period (516 B.C. – 70 A.D.), following the return of the exiles from Babylon, Jewish messianic expectations continued to develop. Although the Jewish people were allowed to return to their land, they remained under the control of foreign powers (Persia, Greece, and eventually Rome). During this time, hopes for a Messiah who would deliver Israel from foreign oppression grew more intense.

The hope for a Davidic king was especially strong among various Jewish groups in the first century A.D. Many Jews expected that the Messiah would be a political and military leader who would overthrow the Roman occupation and restore Israel's sovereignty, much like David had delivered Israel from its enemies and established a united kingdom.

Texts such as the Psalms of Solomon (a Jewish text written in the 1st century B.C.) reflect this expectation of a warrior-Messiah who would defeat Israel's enemies and bring about an era of peace and justice. This expectation was prominent in groups like the Zealots, who sought to violently overthrow Roman rule in the hopes of hastening the arrival of the Messiah.

However, there was also a growing recognition in some circles of Judaism that the Messiah would be more than just a political leader. Some Jewish texts began to speak of the Messiah as a figure who would bring about a new era of spiritual renewal, justice, and peace—ideas that would align closely with Christian understandings of the Messiah.

4. Christian Views of Jesus as the Ultimate Fulfillment of the Messianic Expectation

For Christians, Jesus Christ is the ultimate fulfillment of the Jewish messianic hopes, but His fulfillment of these expectations was radically different from what many Jews of the time anticipated. Rather than being a political or military leader who would deliver Israel from Roman rule, Christians believe that Jesus fulfilled the deeper spiritual aspects of the messianic promises by delivering humanity from sin and death and establishing an eternal kingdom of peace and righteousness.

4.1 Jesus as the Davidic King

The New Testament writers make it clear that Jesus is the fulfillment of the promise of a Davidic king. In the genealogies of Matthew 1 and Luke 3, Jesus is shown to be a direct descendant of David, affirming His rightful claim to the Davidic throne. This is further emphasized in the angel Gabriel's announcement to Mary in Luke 1:32-33:

> "He will be great and will be called the Son of the Most High. And the Lord God will give to him the throne of

his father David, and he will reign over the house of Jacob forever, and of his kingdom there will be no end." (ESV)

Here, the language of eternal kingship echoes the promise made to David in 2 Samuel 7, underscoring the belief that Jesus is the long-awaited Davidic king who would reign forever.

4.2 Jesus as the Righteous Branch

As mentioned earlier, Jeremiah 23:5-6 describes the coming Davidic king as the "Branch of Righteousness." Christians see this prophecy as being fulfilled in Jesus, who is often described as righteous and just in the New Testament. Jesus' teachings, His miracles, and His death and resurrection all demonstrate His embodiment of divine righteousness.

In Romans 3:21-22, the apostle Paul writes:

> "But now the righteousness of God has been manifested apart from the law, although the Law and the Prophets bear witness to it—the righteousness of God through faith in Jesus Christ for all who believe."

Paul emphasizes that Jesus is the manifestation of God's righteousness and that through Him, all who believe are made righteous.

4.3 The Kingdom of God

One of the central aspects of Jesus' ministry was His proclamation of the Kingdom of God. In contrast to the expectation of a political kingdom, Jesus taught that His kingdom was spiritual and transcendent. In Luke 17:20-21, Jesus declares:

> "The kingdom of God is not coming in ways that can be observed, nor will they say, 'Look, here it is!' or 'There!' for behold, the kingdom of

God is in the midst of you."

Through His death and resurrection, Christians believe that Jesus established this eternal kingdom, fulfilling the promises made to David and the prophetic vision of a messianic king who would bring about justice and peace. This kingdom is not confined to one nation but is open to all people, fulfilling the universal scope of God's promises in the Old Testament.

4.4 Jesus as the Good Shepherd

In John 10:11, Jesus refers to Himself as the "Good Shepherd," a direct echo of the messianic imagery found in Ezekiel 34. By identifying Himself as the Good Shepherd, Jesus aligns Himself with the prophetic vision of a Davidic shepherd-king who would care for God's people. This shepherd imagery is central to understanding Jesus' role as the one who leads, protects, and ultimately lays down His life for His people.

5. Conclusion: Jesus as the Ultimate Fulfillment of Jewish Messianic Hope

The Jewish expectation of a Davidic king, rooted in the promises of the Old Testament and developed by the prophets, finds its ultimate fulfillment in the Christian understanding of Jesus Christ. While many Jews expected a political or military leader, Christians believe that Jesus fulfilled the deeper spiritual aspects of the messianic hope by establishing an eternal kingdom of righteousness, justice, and peace.

Through His life, death, and resurrection, Jesus is seen as the embodiment of the righteous Branch, the Good Shepherd, and the Davidic king who reigns forever. For Christians, Jesus' fulfillment of the messianic promises demonstrates not only God's faithfulness to Israel but also His plan for the salvation of all humanity, extending the blessings of the Messiah to all who believe.

The Nature of the Branch

1. Introduction: Understanding "The Lord Our Righteousness"

One of the most striking aspects of Jeremiah's prophecy about the "Branch of Righteousness" is the profound title given to this future king: "The Lord Our Righteousness" (YHWH Tsidkenu). This title suggests that the coming figure would not merely be an earthly ruler from the Davidic line, but one who carries divine significance and acts as the embodiment of God's own righteousness.

In Jeremiah 23:5-6, we read the full prophecy:

> "Behold, the days are coming," declares the LORD, "When I will raise up for David a righteous Branch, and He will reign as king and act wisely and do justice and righteousness in the land. In His days Judah will be saved, and Israel will dwell securely; and this is His name by which He will be called: 'The LORD our righteousness.'" (ESV)

The phrase "The Lord our righteousness" (YHWH Tsidkenu) is key to understanding both the divine nature of the Branch and its implications for Israel's salvation. In this chapter, we will explore the divine aspects of this prophecy, focusing on how the title points to the unique relationship between God, righteousness, and the future Messiah. This exploration will also delve into how Christians see this title as directly linked to the divinity of Jesus Christ.

2. The Meaning of "The Lord Our Righteousness"

The title YHWH Tsidkenu is one of the most profound names given to the Messiah in the Old Testament. To fully appreciate its significance, it is essential to break down the two elements of this title: YHWH and Tsidkenu.

2.1 The Name YHWH

YHWH is the personal name of God, revealed to Moses in Exodus 3:14 when God spoke to him from the burning bush, declaring, "I AM WHO I AM" (Ehyeh-Asher-Ehyeh in Hebrew). This name signifies God's eternal, self-sufficient, and unchanging nature. YHWH is used throughout the Old Testament to refer to the God of Israel, and it carries with it the weight of divine holiness, covenant faithfulness, and authority.

By ascribing the name YHWH to the Branch, Jeremiah is not merely identifying this future king as a descendant of David, but he is also associating this figure with God Himself. This association hints at the divine nature of the Messiah, which is a significant aspect of Christian theology. For Christians, this is seen as a prophecy pointing toward Jesus Christ, who is understood to be both fully human and fully divine—God incarnate.

2.2 The Word Tsidkenu

The Hebrew word Tsidkenu comes from the root tsedek, which means righteousness, justice, or rectitude. It often refers to being morally right or justified, especially in terms of one's relationship with God. The term righteousness in the Old Testament is closely tied to covenant faithfulness, justice, and divine order.

In this context, Tsidkenu refers to the righteousness that the Branch will bring and embody. It is not just the execution of justice as a king but an actual embodiment of divine righteousness. The phrase "The Lord our righteousness" implies that this future king would be the source of righteousness for God's people. He would not only rule with righteousness but also provide it to the people, restoring their relationship with God.

This idea of the Messiah providing righteousness aligns with the broader biblical narrative, particularly in Christian theology, where Jesus is seen as the one through whom believers are justified and made righteous before God.

3. Divine Attributes in "The Lord Our Righteousness"

The title YHWH Tsidkenu points to several divine attributes that the Branch will embody, indicating that this future figure will possess qualities beyond those of a typical earthly king.

3.1 The Branch as the Source of Righteousness

The phrase "The Lord our righteousness" indicates that the Branch will be more than just a righteous ruler; He will be the very source of righteousness for the people. In the Old Testament, righteousness is often depicted as something that belongs to God alone and is given to humanity through obedience to the Law. However, in this prophecy, the Branch is described as the one who brings righteousness directly to the people.

This idea of the Messiah as the source of righteousness is echoed in Christian theology, particularly in 2 Corinthians 5:21, where Paul writes:

> "For our sake He made Him to be sin who knew no sin, so that in Him we might become the righteousness of God." (ESV)

Here, Paul explains that through Jesus' sacrifice, believers receive righteousness—not their own righteousness, but the righteousness of God. This reflects the deeper theological concept that Jesus, as the divine Messiah, provides the righteousness necessary for salvation. This directly correlates with the prophecy in Jeremiah, where the Branch brings righteousness to Judah and Israel, offering security and salvation.

3.2 The Branch as the Divine Savior

In Jeremiah 23:6, it is said that "In His days Judah will be saved, and Israel will dwell securely." This salvation is not merely political or military but is presented as a divine act of deliverance. The fact that this salvation is linked with the name YHWH implies that it is God Himself who is acting through the Branch to save His people.

In Christian thought, this divine salvation is realized in the person of Jesus Christ. The New Testament frequently refers to Jesus as the Savior, who brings salvation not only to Israel but to all humanity. For example, Luke 2:11 declares:

> "For unto you is born this day in the city of David a Savior, who is Christ the Lord." (ESV)

By identifying Jesus as both Savior and Lord, the New Testament affirms the divine nature of Jesus and connects Him with the messianic prophecies in the Old Testament, including Jeremiah's prophecy of the "Branch of Righteousness." Christians believe that Jesus is the ultimate fulfillment of this prophecy because He provides the ultimate salvation and eternal security promised by Jeremiah.

3.3 The Branch as the King of Justice and Peace

Another significant aspect of the prophecy is the idea that the Branch will "act wisely and do justice and righteousness in the land" (Jeremiah 23:5). The combination of wisdom, justice, and righteousness are attributes often ascribed to God in the Old Testament. In Isaiah 9:6-7, another famous messianic prophecy, the coming ruler is described as the "Prince of Peace" whose kingdom will be established with justice and righteousness forever.

The fulfillment of this prophecy is found in the New Testament depiction of Jesus as the ultimate King, whose reign is characterized by divine wisdom, justice, and peace. In the book of Revelation 19:11, Jesus is described as the one who judges and makes war "in righteousness," further aligning with the Old Testament vision of the Messiah as a righteous and wise king.

4. The Role of the Branch in Providing Righteousness

The prophecy of the Branch in Jeremiah 23:5-6 does not simply describe a ruler who exhibits righteousness but speaks of a king who provides righteousness to the people. This concept has deep theological implications in both the Old and New Testaments, as it points to the way in which God restores His people through the Messiah.

4.1 Righteousness and Covenant Relationship

In the Old Testament, righteousness is often tied to the covenant relationship between God and Israel. Righteousness, in this sense, refers to the right standing before God that comes through obedience to His laws. However, Israel and Judah had failed to live up to their covenant obligations, leading to their spiritual and moral downfall. The promise of a righteous Branch indicates that God would intervene to restore this relationship by providing the righteousness that the people could not attain on their own.

In Christian theology, this promise is seen as being fulfilled through Jesus, who offers believers the righteousness necessary to be reconciled to God. Romans 3:22-24 speaks of this righteousness as a gift from God:

> "The righteousness of God through faith in Jesus Christ for all who believe. For there is no distinction: for all have sinned and fall short of the glory of God, and are justified by His grace as a gift, through the redemption that is in Christ Jesus." (ESV)

This passage emphasizes the Christian belief that righteousness is not something earned by human effort but is given through faith in Jesus Christ, the righteous Branch. Through His life, death, and resurrection, Jesus provides the righteousness that restores humanity's broken relationship with God.

4.2 The Imputation of Righteousness

One of the key theological concepts in Christian doctrine is the idea of the imputation of righteousness. This refers to the belief that Jesus' righteousness is credited or imputed to believers through faith. This means that when God looks at believers, He does not see their sin but sees the righteousness of Christ.

This idea is rooted in passages like Jeremiah 23:6, where the Messiah is called "The Lord our righteousness," and further developed in the New Testament. Philippians 3:9 reflects this belief:

> "And be found in Him, not having a righteousness of my own that comes from the law, but that which comes through faith in Christ, the righteousness from God that depends on faith." (ESV)

For Christians, the righteousness provided by Jesus is not just a moral example to follow but a transformative gift that brings believers into a right relationship with God. This righteousness is foundational

to the Christian understanding of salvation, and it directly correlates with Jeremiah's prophecy of the Branch who will be "The Lord our righteousness."

5. Conclusion: The Divine Nature of the Branch

Jeremiah's prophecy of the "Branch of Righteousness" holds profound theological significance, especially when understood in light of the divine title "The Lord our righteousness." This title points not only to the role of the Messiah as a righteous king but also to His divine nature as the embodiment of God's righteousness. By using the name YHWH to describe the Branch, Jeremiah indicates that this future king will be more than just an earthly ruler; He will be God's direct intervention in human history to provide righteousness and salvation for His people.

For Christians, this prophecy finds its ultimate fulfillment in Jesus Christ, who is seen as both the Davidic king and the divine Savior. Jesus, as "The Lord our righteousness," fulfills the promise of righteousness, providing the means by which humanity can be reconciled to God. His life, death, and resurrection bring about the salvation and security promised in Jeremiah, establishing an eternal kingdom of peace, justice, and righteousness.

Thus, the divine nature of the Branch is central to understanding both the messianic hope of the Old Testament and the Christian belief in Jesus as the incarnate Son of God. Through Him, the righteousness of God is made available to all who believe, fulfilling the ancient prophecy and bringing salvation to the world.

CHAPTER 03

____

CONNECTION TO JESUS

1. Introduction: Linking Old Testament Prophecy to Jesus

The New Testament writers consistently link Jesus Christ to the messianic prophecies of the Old Testament, and one of the most significant of these prophecies is found in Jeremiah 23:5-6, which speaks of the "Branch of Righteousness" from the line of David. For the early Christians, understanding Jesus as the fulfillment of these prophecies was crucial to affirming His identity as the Messiah and the Son of God. The title "The Lord our righteousness" ascribed to this future king in Jeremiah's prophecy resonated deeply with the early church, as they saw in Jesus the divine Savior who would bring salvation, righteousness, and the fulfillment of God's promises.

In this chapter, we will explore how the New Testament writers directly and indirectly linked Jeremiah's prophecy of the "Branch of Righteousness" to the life, ministry, and redemptive work of Jesus. By doing so, we will better understand how early Christians viewed Jesus not just as a continuation of Israel's hope but as the ultimate fulfillment of the messianic expectations laid out in the Old Testament.

2. Jesus as the Davidic King

One of the central themes of Jeremiah's prophecy is the promise of a righteous king from the line of David. In Jeremiah 23:5-6, the Lord declares that He will raise up a "righteous Branch" from David's line, signaling the continuation of the Davidic dynasty and the fulfillment of God's covenant with David. The New Testament writers explicitly identify Jesus as this Davidic king, making it clear that He is the long-awaited Messiah who fulfills the promises of the Old Testament.

2.1 The Genealogies of Jesus

Both the Gospels of Matthew and Luke take great care to trace Jesus' genealogy back to David, affirming His royal lineage and His rightful claim to the Davidic throne. In Matthew 1:1, the genealogy opens with the declaration, "The book of the genealogy of Jesus Christ, the son of David, the son of Abraham," immediately linking Jesus to the covenantal promises made to both Abraham and David.

The genealogy in Matthew 1:6 specifically mentions David: "And Jesse the father of David the king. And David was the father of Solomon by the wife of Uriah." This genealogical record not only affirms Jesus' legal claim to the Davidic throne through Joseph but also emphasizes His connection to the prophecies of the Davidic line, including the one found in Jeremiah 23.

Similarly, in Luke 1:32-33, the angel Gabriel announces to Mary that her son will fulfill the role of the Davidic king:

> "He will be great and will be called the Son of the Most High. And the Lord God will give him the throne of his father David, and he will reign over the house of Jacob forever, and of his kingdom there will be no end." (ESV)

This passage directly ties Jesus' kingship to the promises made in the Davidic Covenant (2 Samuel 7:12-16) and echoes Jeremiah's prophecy that the Branch of David will rule with wisdom, righteousness, and justice.

2.2 Jesus Proclaimed as the King of Israel

Throughout the New Testament, Jesus is repeatedly identified as the King of Israel, a fulfillment of the messianic expectation for a Davidic ruler. In John 1:49, Nathanael proclaims Jesus as the King of Israel:

> "Nathanael answered him, 'Rabbi, you are the Son of God! You are the King of Israel!'" (ESV)

By referring to Jesus as the King of Israel, Nathanael acknowledges Jesus' rightful place as the descendant of David and the fulfillment of Jeremiah's prophecy about the Branch of Righteousness.

Moreover, during Jesus' triumphal entry into Jerusalem, the crowds hailed Him as the promised king from David's line. In Matthew 21:9, we read:

> "And the crowds that went before him and that followed him were shouting, 'Hosanna to the Son of David! Blessed is he who comes in the name of the Lord! Hosanna in the highest!'" (ESV)

This moment, celebrated on Palm Sunday, is significant because it shows the people of Jerusalem recognizing Jesus as the Davidic king, directly tying their hope in the Messiah to the Old Testament promises, including those found in Jeremiah 23.

3. Jesus as the Righteous Branch

In Jeremiah 23:5, the future Davidic king is described as a "righteous Branch" who will reign with wisdom and execute justice. For early Christians, Jesus perfectly embodied the righteousness and justice prophesied by Jeremiah, and they often referred to Him in ways that reflect this understanding.

3.1 Jesus as the Embodiment of Righteousness

The righteousness of the Branch in Jeremiah's prophecy is not merely a moral quality but reflects divine righteousness. Jesus is seen as the fulfillment of this aspect of the prophecy, as He embodies perfect righteousness and offers that righteousness to humanity. In the New Testament, Jesus is frequently associated with righteousness, both in His teachings and in the salvation He offers.

In 1 Corinthians 1:30, Paul speaks of Jesus as the source of righteousness for believers:

> "And because of him you are in Christ Jesus, who became to us wisdom from God, righteousness and sanctification and redemption." (ESV)

This passage ties Jesus' role directly to the prophecy of the righteous Branch, as He is identified as the one through whom God's righteousness is made available to humanity. Christians believe that through faith in Jesus, they receive the righteousness that was prophesied in Jeremiah 23.

Similarly, in Romans 3:22, Paul writes:

> "The righteousness of God through faith in Jesus Christ for all who believe." (ESV)

For Paul and other early Christians, the righteousness that the Branch brings is fulfilled in Jesus, whose life, death, and resurrection provide the means by which people are made right with God.

3.2 Jesus and the Ministry of Justice and Salvation

Jeremiah's prophecy also speaks of the Branch who will "do justice and righteousness in the land" and bring salvation to Judah and Israel. Throughout His ministry, Jesus exemplified justice and salvation, not only through His teaching but through His redemptive work on the cross.

In Luke 4:18-19, at the beginning of His public ministry, Jesus announces His mission, quoting from the prophet Isaiah:

> "The Spirit of the Lord is upon me, because he has anointed me to proclaim good news to the poor. He has sent me to proclaim liberty to the captives and recovering of sight to the blind, to set at liberty those who are oppressed, to proclaim the year of the Lord's favor." (ESV)

Here, Jesus emphasizes justice for the oppressed and salvation for the captives, themes that resonate with Jeremiah's prophecy about the righteous Branch. By healing the sick, raising the dead, and offering forgiveness to sinners, Jesus demonstrated the justice and salvation that the Messiah was expected to bring.

4. Jesus as "The Lord Our Righteousness"

One of the most powerful aspects of Jeremiah's prophecy is the title given to the Branch: "The LORD our righteousness" (YHWH Tsidkenu). This title implies both divine and redemptive qualities. For early Christians, this name was a clear indication of Jesus' divine identity and His role in bringing about the righteousness of God.

4.1 The Divine Identity of Jesus

The title "The LORD our righteousness" uses the divine name YHWH, which is significant because it directly associates the Branch with God Himself. In Christian theology, this title is seen as an affirmation of Jesus' divinity. The New Testament writers emphasize that Jesus is not only a descendant of David but also the incarnate Son of God, fully divine and fully human.

In John 1:1, 14, we read about Jesus' divine nature:

> "In the beginning was the Word, and the Word was with God, and the Word was God... And the Word became flesh and dwelt among us, and we have seen his glory, glory as of the only Son from the Father, full of grace and truth." (ESV)

By describing Jesus as "the Word" who "was God" and "became flesh," John affirms the belief that Jesus, as the Messiah, fulfills the divine aspect of Jeremiah's prophecy. He is YHWH Tsidkenu—the Lord who embodies and brings righteousness.

4.2 Jesus as the Provider of Righteousness

For early Christians, one of the key ways Jesus fulfilled the prophecy of the Branch was by providing righteousness to all who believe in Him. This is a central theme in Paul's writings, where he repeatedly emphasizes that righteousness comes through faith in Christ, not through works of the law.

In Philippians 3:9, Paul writes:

> "And be found in him, not having a righteousness of my own that comes from the law, but that which comes through faith in Christ, the righteousness from God that depends on faith." (ESV)

This idea of being made righteous through faith in Jesus is central to Christian soteriology, the doctrine of salvation. Christians believe that through Jesus, they receive the righteousness of God, which was promised in the Old Testament. This aligns directly with Jeremiah's prophecy that the Branch would be called "The LORD our righteousness," as Jesus is understood to be the one who provides the righteousness necessary for salvation.

5. Conclusion: Jesus as the Fulfillment of Jeremiah's Prophecy

For the New Testament writers, the connection between Jeremiah

's prophecy of the "Branch of Righteousness" and the life and ministry of Jesus is clear. Jesus is seen as the Davidic king who fulfills the promises made to Israel, not merely as a political leader but as the divine Savior who embodies righteousness and offers it to all who believe.

Jesus fulfills the divine title "The LORD our righteousness" through His incarnation, life, death, and resurrection, providing the means by which humanity is reconciled to God. In this way, Christians view Jesus as the ultimate fulfillment of Jeremiah's prophecy, the righteous Branch who brings salvation and peace to Israel and the entire world.

The New Covenant

1. Introduction: The Promise of a New Covenant

In Jeremiah 31:31-34, one of the most profound promises of the Old Testament is declared: the coming of a New Covenant between God and His people. This covenant, unlike the one made at Sinai, would be internal and transformative, written on the hearts of God's people rather than on tablets of stone. For Christians, this passage holds immense theological significance because they believe that Jesus Christ instituted this New Covenant through His life, death, and resurrection. The New Testament, particularly the Book of Hebrews, emphasizes that Jesus is the mediator of this New Covenant, fulfilling the promises made through Jeremiah and bringing about a new era in the relationship between God and humanity.

The concept of the New Covenant marks a turning point in the biblical narrative, transitioning from the external regulations of the Mosaic Law to the internal transformation that comes through the work of the Holy Spirit. In this chapter, we will explore the significance of the New Covenant as presented in Jeremiah, its fulfillment in the life and work of Jesus, and how the New Testament writers understood this covenant in relation to the broader story of salvation.

2. The Old Covenant: Its Nature and Limitations

To fully appreciate the significance of the New Covenant, it is essential to understand the nature of the Old Covenant, which was established between God and the people of Israel at Mount Sinai. This covenant, often referred to as the Mosaic Covenant, was based on the Law that God gave to Moses, which included the Ten Commandments and the various ceremonial, moral, and civil laws that governed Israel's relationship with God and one another.

2.1 The Covenant at Sinai

The Old Covenant was a binding agreement that God made with Israel after delivering them from slavery in Egypt. In Exodus 19:5-6, God makes the terms of the covenant clear:

> "Now therefore, if you will indeed obey my voice and keep my covenant, you shall be my treasured possession among all peoples, for all the earth is mine; and you shall be to me a kingdom of priests and a holy nation." (ESV)

The covenant was conditional, dependent on Israel's obedience to God's laws. Israel was called to be a holy nation, set apart from other peoples, and their continued blessing and relationship with God depended on their adherence to the covenant.

2.2 The Law and the Covenant

The heart of the Old Covenant was the Law, which God gave to Israel as both a guide for righteous living and a means to maintain fellowship with Him. However, the Law also revealed humanity's inability to fully live up to God's standards. Time and again, Israel failed to keep the terms of the covenant, turning to idolatry and disobedience. The prophet Jeremiah repeatedly laments Israel's faithlessness, describing how they have broken the covenant made with God.

In Jeremiah 11:10, God says:

> "They have turned back to the iniquities of their forefathers, who refused to hear my words. They have gone after other gods to serve them. The house of Israel and the house of Judah have broken my covenant that I made with their fathers." (ESV)

This failure highlighted the limitations of the Old Covenant. While the Law was perfect and holy, it could not transform the hearts of the people. Israel's continual disobedience revealed the need for a deeper, more transformative covenant—one that would address the internal condition of the human heart.

3. The Prophecy of the New Covenant

Against the backdrop of Israel's failure to keep the Old Covenant, Jeremiah offers a remarkable prophecy of hope and renewal. In Jeremiah 31:31-34, God speaks of a New Covenant that will not be like the one made at Sinai but will bring about a profound internal transformation in His people:

> "Behold, the days are coming, declares the LORD, when I will make a new covenant with the house of Israel and the house of Judah, not like the covenant that I made with their fathers on the day when I took them by the hand to bring them out of the land of Egypt, my covenant that they broke, though I was their husband, declares the LORD. But this is

the covenant that I will make with the house of Israel after those days, declares the LORD: I will put my law within them, and I will write it on their hearts. And I will be their God, and they shall be my people. And no longer shall each one teach his neighbor and each his brother, saying, 'Know the LORD,' for they shall all know me, from the least of them to the greatest, declares the LORD. For I will forgive their iniquity, and I will remember their sin no more." (ESV)

This passage is revolutionary because it shifts the focus from external laws and rituals to an internal, heart-centered relationship between God and His people. The key features of this New Covenant are:

3.1 An Internal Law

Unlike the Old Covenant, where the law was written on stone tablets, the New Covenant promises that God's law will be written on the hearts of His people. This implies a transformation of the inner person, where obedience to God is no longer an external obligation but flows from a renewed heart. This internalization of God's law points to the work of the Holy Spirit, who, according to Christian theology, indwells believers and empowers them to live in obedience to God.

3.2 A Personal Relationship with God

In the New Covenant, God promises that all His people will know Him personally. This knowledge is not merely intellectual but relational and experiential. In the Old Covenant, the people relied on priests and mediators to represent them before God, but the New Covenant promises direct access to God for all His people, "from the least of them to the greatest." This democratization of access to God reflects the intimate relationship God desires to have with His people.

3.3 Forgiveness of Sins

One of the most significant aspects of the New Covenant is the promise of forgiveness: "For I will forgive their iniquity, and I will remember their sin no more." Under the Old Covenant, forgiveness was temporary and required repeated sacrifices. But in the New Covenant, God promises complete and lasting forgiveness of sins, a promise that Christians believe is fulfilled through the sacrifice of Jesus Christ.

4. The Fulfillment of the New Covenant in Jesus

Christians believe that Jesus Christ is the mediator of the New Covenant, fulfilling the prophecy in Jeremiah through His life, death, and resurrection. The New Testament repeatedly identifies Jesus as the one who brings the New Covenant into reality, and His sacrifice on the cross is seen as the means by which the New Covenant is established.

4.1 Jesus' Institution of the New Covenant

The clearest connection between Jesus and the New Covenant is found in the accounts of the Last Supper, where Jesus explicitly refers to His impending death as the institution of the New Covenant. In Luke 22:20, Jesus says:

> "And likewise the cup after they had eaten, saying, 'This cup that is poured out for you is the new covenant in my blood.'" (ESV)

By referring to His blood as the basis of the New Covenant, Jesus connects His sacrificial death with the promises made in Jeremiah 31. His death on the cross is understood by Christians as the ultimate act of atonement, providing the forgiveness of sins promised in the New Covenant.

4.2 The Book of Hebrews and the New Covenant

The Book of Hebrews provides the most extensive theological reflection on the New Covenant and its fulfillment in Jesus. Hebrews portrays Jesus as the great High Priest and the mediator of a better covenant, one that surpasses the Old Covenant in every way. In Hebrews 8:6-7, we read:

> "But as it is, Christ has obtained a ministry that is as much more excellent than the old as the covenant he mediates is better, since it is enacted on better promises. For if that first covenant had been faultless, there would have been no occasion to look for a second." (ESV)

The author of Hebrews directly quotes Jeremiah 31:31-34 in Hebrews 8:8-12, arguing that the New Covenant has been fulfilled in Jesus and that His once-for-all sacrifice replaces the repeated animal sacrifices of the Old Covenant. Through Jesus, believers experience the internal transformation and forgiveness that Jeremiah promised.

4.3 The Holy Spirit and the New Covenant

The promise of an internal law written on the hearts of God's people is fulfilled in Christian theology through the indwelling of the Holy Spirit. In the New Testament, the Holy Spirit is described as the agent of transformation who enables believers to live according to God's will. In 2 Corinthians 3:3, Paul writes:

> "And you show that you are a letter from Christ delivered by us, written not with ink but with the Spirit of the living God, not on tablets of stone but on tablets of human hearts." (ESV)

This imagery directly echoes Jeremiah's prophecy, where God promises to write His law on the hearts of His people. The Holy Spirit plays a central role in the New Covenant, enabling believers to live in a new relationship with God, marked by obedience, intimacy, and forgiveness.

5. The New Covenant and Christian Life

For Christians, living under the New Covenant means experiencing a transformed relationship with God, characterized by forgiveness, direct access to God, and the indwelling presence of the Holy Spirit. The New Covenant redefines what it means to be in covenant with God, shifting the focus from external rituals to a heart-oriented faith.

5.1 Forgiveness and Reconciliation

The New Covenant, as established through Jesus, offers full and final forgiveness of sins. This forgiveness is not contingent on repeated sacrifices, as in the Old Covenant, but is secured through the once-for-all sacrifice of Jesus. Christians believe that through faith in Jesus, they are reconciled to God and can live in the assurance of God's grace and mercy.

5.2 The Law Written on Hearts

The internalization of God's law is one of the hallmarks of the New Covenant. Christians believe that the Holy Spirit empowers them to live in accordance with God's will, not out of mere obligation but out of a transformed heart. This inward transformation reflects the deep intimacy of the New Covenant relationship, where obedience to God is an act of love and worship rather than external compliance.

5.3 The Universal Scope of the New Covenant

While Jeremiah's prophecy was initially directed at the house of Israel and Judah, the New Covenant is understood in Christian theology to extend beyond ethnic Israel to include all people. Through Jesus, the New Covenant is offered to all nations, fulfilling God's promise to bless all the families of the earth. As Paul writes in Galatians 3:28-29:

> "There is neither Jew nor Greek, there is neither slave nor free, there is no male and female, for you are all one in Christ Jesus. And if you are Christ's, then you are Abraham's offspring, heirs according to promise." (ESV)

This universal aspect of the New Covenant reflects the expansion of God's plan of salvation, where all who believe in Jesus are brought into the family of God and experience the blessings of the New Covenant.

6. Conclusion: The Fulfillment of the New Covenant in Jesus

The prophecy of the New Covenant in Jeremiah 31:31-34 is one of the most significant promises in the Old Testament, offering hope for a future in which God's people would experience a transformed relationship with Him. For Christians, this promise is fulfilled in Jesus Christ, who established the New Covenant through His death and resurrection. Jesus, as the mediator of the New Covenant, brings forgiveness of sins, writes God's law on the hearts of believers, and offers a direct, personal relationship with God.

The New Covenant represents a profound shift in the way humanity relates to God, moving from external regulations to an internal transformation through the Holy Spirit. For Christians, living under the New Covenant means experiencing the grace and mercy of God through Jesus Christ, and it provides the assurance of forgiveness, intimacy with God, and the promise of eternal life. Thus, the New Covenant stands as a central pillar of Christian theology, embodying the fulfillment of God's redemptive plan for humanity.

The Old Covenant vs. The New Covenant

1. Introduction: The Shift from the Old Covenant to the New Covenant

The Old Covenant, often referred to as the Mosaic Covenant, is central to the history of Israel's relationship with God. This covenant, established at Mount Sinai, laid the foundation for how the Israelites were to live, worship, and relate to God. However, as the Old Testament narratives unfold, it becomes clear that the Mosaic Covenant, while holy and good, had significant limitations due to human sinfulness. These limitations created the need for a New Covenant, one that would address the shortcomings of the old system and provide a lasting solution to humanity's separation from God.

In Jeremiah 31:31-34, the prophet foretells a New Covenant that would be different from the one made with the Israelites at Sinai. This New Covenant would address the inherent weaknesses of the Old Covenant and establish a deeper, more intimate relationship between God and His people. For Christians, this New Covenant is fulfilled through Jesus Christ, whose life, death, and resurrection bring about a transformative relationship with God that transcends the limitations of the Mosaic Covenant.

In this chapter, we will explore the key differences between the Old and New Covenants, the limitations of the Mosaic Law, and the theological reasons for the establishment of the New Covenant.

2. The Old Covenant: Structure and Purpose

2.1 The Mosaic Covenant

The Old Covenant was formally established between God and the people of Israel at Mount Sinai after their exodus from Egypt. It is referred to as the Mosaic Covenant because Moses was the mediator between God and the Israelites during this pivotal event. The essence of this covenant was captured in the giving of the Law, which included the Ten Commandments, as well as various ceremonial, moral, and civil regulations designed to govern Israel's relationship with God and one another.

In Exodus 19:5-6, God laid out the terms of this covenant:

> "Now therefore, if you will indeed obey my voice and keep my covenant, you shall be my treasured possession among all peoples, for all the earth is mine; and you shall be to me a kingdom of priests and a holy nation." (ESV)

This covenant was conditional and based on obedience. Israel was called to be a holy nation, set apart from the surrounding peoples. In return for their obedience, God promised to bless them, protect them, and dwell among them.

2.2 The Purpose of the Mosaic Law

The Law given through Moses had several key purposes:

- To Reflect God's Holiness: The Law was a reflection of God's holiness and righteousness. It was designed to set Israel apart from other nations as a people who lived according to God's standards.

- To Regulate Worship and Life: The ceremonial and sacrificial aspects of the Law regulated how the Israelites were to worship God. It also provided guidelines for living in community, promoting justice, mercy, and love toward one another.

- To Serve as a Covenant Sign: The Law served as the sign of the covenant between God and Israel. By keeping the Law, the Israelites demonstrated their loyalty and commitment to God.

- To Expose Sin: The Law also had the function of exposing sin. Paul writes in Romans 7:7 that the Law revealed the true nature of sin: "Yet if it had not been for the law, I would not have known sin. For I would not have known what it is to covet if the law had not said, 'You shall not covet.'" (ESV)

While the Mosaic Law was good and served as a guide for righteous living, it had inherent limitations due to human sinfulness. These limitations underscored the need for a New Covenant that would go beyond the external regulations of the Law.

3. The Limitations of the Old Covenant

Despite its divine origin, the Old Covenant had several limitations that made it ineffective as a permanent solution to humanity's problem of sin and estrangement from God. The primary limitations of the Mosaic Covenant can be summarized as follows:

3.1 External Law

One of the most significant limitations of the Old Covenant was its external nature. The Mosaic Law was written on stone tablets and required adherence to external rules and rituals. While the Law could guide behavior, it could not change the human heart. The Law revealed what righteousness looked like, but it did not have the power to enable people to live righteously from within.

Jeremiah highlighted this problem in Jeremiah 17:9, where he describes the condition of the human heart:

> "The heart is deceitful above all things, and desperately sick; who can understand it?" (ESV)

This deep-rooted sinfulness meant that the people of Israel were incapable of fully keeping the Law, even though they might strive to follow its precepts externally.

3.2 The Problem of Human Disobedience

The Old Covenant was based on conditional promises—if Israel obeyed, they would experience blessings, but if they disobeyed, they would face curses and punishment (Deuteronomy 28). However, Israel's history is one of repeated disobedience and covenant breaking. Time and again, the people turned away from God to worship idols and follow their own desires.

Jeremiah points out the failure of the people to keep the covenant in Jeremiah 11:10:

> "They have turned back to the iniquities of their forefathers, who refused to hear my words. They have gone

after other gods to serve them. The house of Israel and the house of Judah have broken my covenant that I made with their fathers." (ESV)

The repeated disobedience of Israel demonstrated the inadequacy of the Old Covenant to produce lasting faithfulness to God. The people's inability to uphold their end of the covenant highlighted the need for a new approach—one that addressed the problem of human sinfulness more effectively.

3.3 Temporary Sacrifices for Sin

Another major limitation of the Old Covenant was its sacrificial system. Under the Mosaic Law, animal sacrifices were required to atone for the sins of the people. However, these sacrifices were temporary and needed to be repeated continually. The blood of animals could not fully cleanse people from sin but only provided a temporary covering. In Hebrews 10:1, the writer explains:

> "For since the law has but a shadow of the good things to come instead of the true form of these realities, it can never, by the same sacrifices that are continually offered every year, make perfect those who draw near." (ESV)

The sacrificial system of the Old Covenant pointed forward to a greater sacrifice—one that would provide permanent forgiveness and cleansing from sin.

3.4 Lack of Internal Transformation

Perhaps the most significant limitation of the Old Covenant was its inability to transform the hearts of the people. While the Law could instruct and reveal sin, it could not provide the power to live in true obedience to God. This lack of internal transformation meant that the people were constantly falling into cycles of disobedience and repentance, never fully able to maintain the covenant relationship with God.

As a result of these limitations, the Old Covenant was unable to bring about the full restoration and redemption that humanity needed. The Law was good, but it could not overcome the problem of sin at its root. This reality created the need for a New Covenant—one that would address the internal condition of the human heart and provide a lasting solution to sin and separation from God.

4. The New Covenant: Addressing the Limitations of the Old

The New Covenant, as prophesied by Jeremiah, was designed to address the limitations of the Old Covenant and provide a permanent, transformative solution to humanity's problem of sin. In Jeremiah 31:31-34, God promises to establish a New Covenant that would fundamentally change the relationship between God and His people:

> "Behold, the days are coming, declares the LORD, when I will make a new covenant with the house of Israel and the house of Judah… For this is the covenant that I will make with the house of Israel after those days, declares the LORD: I will put my law within them, and I will write it on their hearts. And I will be their God, and they shall be my people… For I will forgive their iniquity, and I will remember their sin no more." (ESV)

4.1 The Law Written on Hearts

One of the key features of the New Covenant is that God's law would no longer be external but would be written on the hearts of His people. This promise signifies a profound internal transformation, where obedience to God would come from a changed heart rather than mere external conformity. The New Covenant addresses the problem of the human heart by providing the internal renewal necessary for true obedience to God's will.

In Christian theology, this internal transformation is accomplished through the indwelling of the Holy Spirit. Paul explains in 2 Corinthians 3:3:

> "And you show that you are a letter from Christ delivered by us, written not with ink but with the Spirit of the living God, not on tablets of stone but on tablets of human hearts." (ESV)

The Holy Spirit empowers believers to live in accordance with God's will, fulfilling the promise of the New Covenant that the law would be written on their hearts.

4.2 Personal Knowledge of God

Another feature of the New Covenant is the promise of a personal relationship with God. Under the Old Covenant, access to God was mediated through priests, and the people often felt distant from God. However, in the New Covenant, God promises that "they shall all know me, from the least of them to the greatest." This knowledge is relational and intimate, reflecting the closeness that God desires to have with His people.

This personal relationship with God is made possible through Jesus Christ, who, as the mediator of the New Covenant, provides direct access to the Father. In Hebrews 4:16, believers are encouraged to approach God with confidence:

> "Let us then with confidence draw near to the throne of grace, that we may receive mercy and find grace to help in time of need." (ESV)

This access to God is one of the central benefits of the New Covenant, where every believer can experience a direct, personal relationship with their Creator.

4.3 Complete Forgiveness of Sins

Perhaps the most significant aspect of the New Covenant is the promise of complete and lasting forgiveness of sins. In Jeremiah 31:34, God declares, "For I will forgive their iniquity, and I will remember their sin no more." This forgiveness is not temporary, as it was under the Old Covenant, but is permanent and complete.

Christians believe that this forgiveness is made possible through the sacrificial death of Jesus Christ. As the ultimate sacrifice, Jesus' death on the cross provides atonement for sin once and for all. In Hebrews 10:12, it is written:

> "But when Christ had offered for all time a single sacrifice for sins, he sat down at the right hand of God." (ESV)

Jesus' sacrifice fulfills the requirements of the Old Covenant's sacrificial system and brings about the full and final forgiveness of sins, as promised in the New Covenant.

5. The Need for the New Covenant

The limitations of the Old Covenant, combined with humanity's inability to live in perfect obedience to God's law, created the need for a New Covenant. The Mosaic Law, while good and holy, could not address the fundamental problem of sin and the need for internal transformation. The New Covenant, however, provides the solution by offering:

- Internal Transformation: Through the work of the Holy Spirit, believers are transformed from the inside out, enabling them to live in true obedience to God.

- Direct Access to God: The New Covenant offers a personal relationship with God, where all people can know Him intimately and experience His presence.

- Complete Forgiveness: Through the sacrifice of Jesus Christ, the New Covenant brings complete and lasting forgiveness of sins, eliminating the need for repeated sacrifices.

In Christian theology, the New Covenant is understood as the fulfillment of God's redemptive plan, where the limitations of the Old Covenant are overcome, and the relationship between God and humanity is restored through Jesus Christ.

6. Conclusion: The Superiority of the New Covenant

The Old Covenant, established at Sinai, served an essential purpose in revealing God's holiness and exposing the problem of human sinfulness. However, its limitations—external regulations, human disobedience, and temporary sacrifices—necessitated a New Covenant, one that would address the root problem of sin and provide a permanent solution. The New Covenant, as prophesied by Jeremiah and fulfilled through Jesus Christ, surpasses the Old Covenant in every way. It offers internal transformation, personal knowledge of God, and complete forgiveness of sins, bringing about a restored relationship between God and humanity.

For Christians, the New Covenant represents the culmination of God's plan to redeem His people, offering a way of salvation that is not based on human effort but on the grace of God through Jesus Christ. In this way, the New Covenant fulfills the hopes and promises of the Old Testament and brings about a new era of peace, righteousness, and reconciliation with God.

Jesus and the New Covenant

1. Introduction: Jesus as the Fulfillment of the New Covenant

The New Covenant prophesied by Jeremiah in Jeremiah 31:31-34 represents a transformative shift in the relationship between God and His people. Unlike the Old Covenant, which was based on external laws and sacrifices, the New Covenant promised internal transformation, personal knowledge of God, and complete forgiveness of sins. For Christians, the life, death, and resurrection of Jesus Christ mark the fulfillment of this prophecy. Through His teachings, sacrificial death on the cross, and resurrection, Jesus inaugurated the New Covenant, bringing about the spiritual renewal that Jeremiah foretold.

This chapter will explore how Jesus' ministry, death, and resurrection fulfilled Jeremiah's prophecy of the New Covenant, transforming the relationship between God and humanity and establishing a new era of salvation, grace, and redemption.

2. Jesus' Teachings: The Kingdom of God and the Internalization of the Law

One of the key features of the New Covenant prophesied by Jeremiah was the promise that God's law would be written on the hearts of His people rather than merely being external rules written on stone. Jesus' teachings during His earthly ministry emphasized this shift from external obedience to internal transformation. He frequently taught that true righteousness comes from within and that the heart must be aligned with God's will.

2.1 The Sermon on the Mount: Internalizing the Law

In the Sermon on the Mount (Matthew 5-7), Jesus reinterpreted the Mosaic Law in a way that internalized its demands, emphasizing the spirit of the law rather than mere external adherence. Jesus did not abolish the Old Covenant law but fulfilled and deepened its meaning by calling for righteousness that exceeds the external observance of rules.

For example, in Matthew 5:21-22, Jesus says:

> "You have heard that it was said to those of old, 'You shall not murder; and whoever murders will be liable to judgment.' But I say to you that everyone who is angry with his brother will be liable to judgment." (ESV)

Here, Jesus highlights that it is not just the act of murder that violates God's will but the internal attitude of anger. Similarly, in Matthew 5:27-28, He extends the commandment against adultery to include even lustful thoughts. Jesus' teachings emphasized that the true fulfillment of the law involves a transformation of the heart—precisely what Jeremiah's New Covenant promised.

This internalization of the law is further reflected in Matthew 22:37-40, where Jesus summarizes the law as love for God and love for neighbor:

> "And he said to him, 'You shall love the Lord your God with all your heart and with all your soul and with all your mind. This is the great and first commandment. And a second is like it: You shall love your neighbor as yourself. On these two commandments depend all the Law and the Prophets.'" (ESV)

By teaching that the essence of the law is love—an internal orientation of the heart toward God and others—Jesus was laying the foundation for the New Covenant, where the law would be written on the hearts of believers through the work of the Holy Spirit.

2.2 The Kingdom of God: A New Relationship with God

Throughout His ministry, Jesus proclaimed the arrival of the Kingdom of God—a new era of God's rule in which people would live in direct, personal relationship with Him. This message ties closely to Jeremiah's prophecy that, under the New Covenant, "they shall all know me, from the least of them to the greatest" (Jeremiah 31:34).

Jesus' teachings emphasized that the Kingdom of God was not just a future political reality but a present spiritual reality that transforms the hearts and lives of those who enter into it. In Luke 17:20-21, Jesus says:

> "The kingdom of God is not coming in ways that can be observed, nor will they say, 'Look, here it is!' or 'There!' for behold, the kingdom of God is in the midst of you." (ESV)

By establishing the Kingdom of God in the hearts of His followers, Jesus initiated the New Covenant's promise of a personal, intimate relationship with God. This was a radical departure from the Old Covenant's focus on external rituals and regulations and marked the beginning of a new era in the relationship between God and His people.

3. Jesus' Death: The Sacrifice That Established the New Covenant

The New Covenant promised not only internal transformation but also the complete forgiveness of sins. This forgiveness is central to the New Covenant, as God declared through Jeremiah, "For I will forgive their iniquity, and I will remember their sin no more" (Jeremiah 31:34). Christians believe that this promise was fulfilled through Jesus' sacrificial death on the cross.

3.1 The Institution of the New Covenant at the Last Supper

The connection between Jesus' death and the New Covenant is most explicitly made during the Last Supper, where Jesus instituted the sacrament of the Eucharist (or Communion) and declared that His death would establish the New Covenant. In Luke 22:19-20, Jesus says:

> "And he took bread, and when he had given thanks, he broke it and gave it to them, saying, 'This is my body, which is given for you. Do this in remembrance of me.' And likewise the cup after they had eaten, saying, 'This cup that is poured out for you is the new covenant in my blood.'" (ESV)

By referring to His blood as the foundation of the New Covenant, Jesus directly connects His sacrificial death to the promises of forgiveness and transformation outlined in

Jeremiah 31. Just as the Old Covenant was established through the blood of animal sacrifices (Exodus 24:8), the New Covenant is established through the shedding of Jesus' blood, which provides the final and perfect atonement for sin.

3.2 Jesus' Death as the Atonement for Sin

The New Covenant promised complete and lasting forgiveness of sins, something that the Old Covenant could not fully provide. Under the Old Covenant, the sacrificial system required repeated offerings of animals to temporarily cover the sins of the people. However, these sacrifices could never fully remove sin or cleanse the conscience. In contrast, Jesus' death on the cross is seen in Christian theology as the ultimate and final sacrifice that provides total forgiveness and reconciliation with God.

In Hebrews 9:12, the writer explains the significance of Jesus' sacrifice:

> "He entered once for all into the holy places, not by means of the blood of goats and calves but by means of his own blood, thus securing an eternal redemption." (ESV)

By offering His own life, Jesus accomplished what the Old Covenant sacrifices could not—permanent forgiveness and the removal of sin. This is why the writer of Hebrews refers to Jesus as the "mediator of a new covenant" (Hebrews

9:15), fulfilling Jeremiah's prophecy and providing a way for humanity to be restored to a right relationship with God.

4. Jesus' Resurrection: The Inauguration of New Life in the New Covenant

While Jesus' death is central to the establishment of the New Covenant, His resurrection is equally vital in bringing the promises of the New Covenant to full fruition. Jesus' resurrection not only vindicates His identity as the Messiah but also inaugurates the new life that believers experience under the New Covenant.

4.1 The Resurrection as the Confirmation of the New Covenant

Jesus' resurrection from the dead serves as a divine confirmation that His death was an acceptable and sufficient sacrifice for the forgiveness of sins. It is the ultimate proof that the promises of the New Covenant have been fulfilled. In Romans 4:25, Paul writes:

> "He was delivered up for our trespasses and raised for our justification." (ESV)

The resurrection is a declaration that Jesus' atoning work on the cross was successful, providing justification (or righteousness) for all who believe in Him. This justification is the fulfillment of the New Covenant promise that God's people would be made righteous and forgiven of their sins.

4.2 New Life in the Spirit

In addition to confirming the forgiveness of sins, Jesus' resurrection also inaugurates the new life promised in the New Covenant. This new life is marked by the indwelling of the Holy Spirit, who empowers believers to live according to God's will and internalizes the law within their hearts, as promised in Jeremiah 31:33: "I will put my law within them, and I will write it on their hearts."

Jesus' resurrection and ascension led to the outpouring of the Holy Spirit at Pentecost, as recorded in Acts 2. The coming of the Holy Spirit is seen as the fulfillment of the New Covenant's promise of internal transformation. In Romans 8:2-4, Paul explains how the Spirit empowers believers to live out the righteousness of the law:

> "For the law of the Spirit of life has set you free in Christ Jesus from the law of sin and death... in order that the righteous requirement of the law might be fulfilled in us, who walk not according to the flesh but according to the Spirit." (ESV)

Through the resurrection and the gift of the Holy Spirit, believers are enabled to live in the new reality of the New Covenant, where the law is no longer an external code but is written on their hearts.

5. The Ongoing Impact of the New Covenant

The fulfillment of the New Covenant in Jesus' death and resurrection has ongoing implications for Christian life and theology. Believers live in the reality of the New Covenant, enjoying a transformed relationship with God that is characterized by grace, forgiveness, and empowerment through the Holy Spirit.

5.1 Direct Access to God

Under the Old Covenant, access to God was mediated by priests, and only the high priest could enter the Holy of Holies once a year to offer sacrifices for the people's sins. However, the New Covenant, established by Jesus, grants all believers direct access to God. In Hebrews 10:19-22, the writer encourages believers to approach God with confidence:

> "Therefore, brothers, since we have confidence to enter the holy places by the blood of Jesus... let us draw near with a true heart in full assurance of faith." (ESV)

This direct access to God is a hallmark of the New Covenant, where all believers, regardless of their status or background, can have a personal relationship with God.

5.2 The Universal Scope of the New Covenant

While Jeremiah's prophecy was initially addressed to Israel and Judah, Christians believe that the New Covenant extends beyond ethnic Israel to include all nations. Jesus'

Great Commission in Matthew 28:19-20 reflects this universal scope:

> "Go therefore and make disciples of all nations, baptizing them in the name of the Father and of the Son and of the Holy Spirit, teaching them to observe all that I have commanded you." (ESV)

The New Covenant is open to all who believe in Jesus, fulfilling God's promise to bless all the nations of the earth through Abraham's offspring (Genesis 12:3).

6. Conclusion: Jesus as the Mediator and Fulfillment of the New Covenant

Jeremiah's prophecy of a New Covenant is central to Christian theology, and for Christians, Jesus is the ultimate fulfillment of that prophecy. Through His teachings, Jesus emphasized the internalization of God's law and a personal relationship with God. Through His sacrificial death on the cross, He established the New Covenant, offering complete forgiveness of sins. And through His resurrection, He inaugurated new life for all who believe in Him, empowered by the Holy Spirit to live in accordance with God's will.

For Christians, the New Covenant is not just a future promise but a present reality, one that defines their relationship with God and offers the assurance of salvation, forgiveness, and eternal life. In this way, Jesus stands as the mediator and fulfillment of the New Covenant, bringing about the transformation and redemption that Jeremiah prophesied centuries before.

The Law Written on Hearts

1. Introduction: Spiritual Transformation in the New Covenant

In Jeremiah 31:33, the prophet reveals one of the most profound promises of the New Covenant: the transformation of the heart. God declares:

> "I will put my law within them, and I will write it on their hearts. And I will be their God, and they shall be my people." (ESV)

This passage signifies a shift from the Old Covenant's external adherence to the Mosaic Law, inscribed on stone tablets, to an internal transformation that would enable God's people to live in alignment with His will. Instead of merely following regulations, under the New Covenant, God's people would have His law inscribed on their hearts, shaping their desires, values, and actions from within.

For Christians, this promise is fulfilled through the work of Jesus Christ and the indwelling of the Holy Spirit. This chapter will explore the nature of this spiritual transformation, how it contrasts with the limitations of the

Old Covenant, and the role of the Holy Spirit in writing God's law on the hearts of believers, empowering them to live in a new relationship with God.

2. The Law of the Old Covenant: External Regulations

To understand the significance of the law being written on hearts, it is essential to grasp how the law functioned under the Old Covenant. The Mosaic Law, given at Mount Sinai, was a set of external regulations meant to govern the moral, ceremonial, and civil life of Israel. It served as a guide for righteousness and was intended to set Israel apart as a holy nation before God.

2.1 The External Nature of the Law

The Mosaic Law was external in nature. It was written on stone tablets and communicated through Moses, dictating how the people should act, worship, and live in community. While the law was perfect in its reflection of God's holiness, it was fundamentally outside of the people. The law showed them what righteousness looked like, but it could not transform their hearts or give them the power to fully live in obedience.

In Deuteronomy 30:10, Moses emphasized the importance of obeying God's commands:

> "When you obey the voice of the LORD your God, to keep his commandments and his statutes that are written in this Book of the Law, when you turn to the LORD your God with all your heart and with all your soul." (ESV)

Despite the call for wholehearted obedience, Israel repeatedly struggled to keep the law. This struggle stemmed from the fact that while the law could instruct behavior, it could not change the inward disposition of the people. As a result, Israel's history under the Old Covenant was marked by cycles of disobedience, repentance, and judgment.

2.2 The Limitations of External Law

The Old Covenant revealed humanity's inability to live up to God's righteous standards. The law was good, but human sinfulness made it impossible to fully comply with its demands. The external nature of the law—written on tablets, carried out through rituals, and enforced through rules—could not address the deeper issue: the sinfulness of the human heart.

In Jeremiah 17:9, the prophet laments the condition of the human heart:

> "The heart is deceitful above all things, and desperately sick; who can understand it?" (ESV)

The law could identify sin but not cure the underlying condition. As Paul explains in Romans 7:7, the law exposed sin: "If it had not been for the law, I would not have known sin." However, the law lacked the power to deliver humanity from sin. This limitation led to the need for a New Covenant, one that would transform people from the inside out, healing the heart and empowering a new kind of obedience.

3. The Promise of a New Covenant: Internal Transformation

In response to Israel's failure to keep the Old Covenant, God promises a New Covenant through the prophet Jeremiah. This New Covenant would be different, for it would address the heart of the problem—human sinfulness—by transforming the heart itself. The key to this transformation is God's promise to write His law on the hearts of His people, signifying a radical internalization of His will.

3.1 The Law Written on Hearts

In Jeremiah 31:33, God makes a profound promise to His people:

> "For this is the covenant that I will make with the house of Israel after those days, declares the LORD: I will put my law within them, and I will write it on their hearts. And I will be their God, and they shall be my people." (ESV)

This promise of internalizing the law is at the heart of the New Covenant. Instead of external rules and regulations,

God's law would become an integral part of the believer's heart, mind, and will. This transformation would not merely change behavior but would reshape the person's very identity, inclinations, and desires.

The internalization of the law is transformative in two key ways:

- A New Disposition Toward God's Will: Instead of struggling against an external code, God's people would have a new desire to follow His will. The law written on the heart signifies an alignment of the believer's desires with God's purposes. Obedience would come not from compulsion but from a genuine, inward desire to please God.

- A Restored Relationship with God: God's promise to write His law on the hearts of His people reflects a deeper, more intimate relationship. As Jeremiah proclaims, "I will be their God, and they shall be my people." This covenant relationship is not based on legal adherence but on a transformed heart that delights in God's presence and seeks to live in accordance with His ways.

3.2 Ezekiel's Vision: A New Heart and Spirit

The promise of internal transformation is echoed in the prophecy of Ezekiel, who envisions a time when God will replace the people's stony, disobedient hearts with hearts of flesh—hearts that are responsive to His will. In Ezekiel 36:26-27, God declares:

> "And I will give you a new heart, and a new spirit I will put within you. And I will remove the heart of stone from your flesh and give you a heart of flesh. And I will put my Spirit within you, and cause you to walk in my statutes and be careful to obey my rules." (ESV)

Here, Ezekiel further clarifies how this transformation will take place: through the giving of God's Spirit. The indwelling presence of the Holy Spirit would be the means by which God writes His law on the hearts of His people, enabling them to live in obedience and faithfulness.

4. The Role of the Holy Spirit in the New Covenant

In Christian theology, the promise of the law being written on the heart is fulfilled through the indwelling of the Holy Spirit. The Holy Spirit plays a central role in the New Covenant by enabling believers to live according to God's will, empowering them to experience the spiritual transformation that was impossible under the Old Covenant.

4.1 The Indwelling of the Holy Spirit

One of the defining features of the New Covenant is that the Holy Spirit comes to dwell within believers, making possible the internal transformation promised by Jeremiah and Ezekiel. In John 14:16-17, Jesus speaks of the coming of the Holy Spirit:

> "And I will ask the Father, and he will give you another Helper, to be with you forever, even the Spirit of truth... You know him, for he dwells with you and will be in you." (ESV)

The Holy Spirit's indwelling presence fulfills the promise of the New Covenant, as the Spirit writes God's law on the hearts of believers, guiding them into truth and enabling them to live out God's commandments.

4.2 The Holy Spirit as the Source of Obedience

The Holy Spirit not only convicts believers of sin and brings about repentance but also empowers them to live in obedience to God's will. The internal transformation wrought by the Spirit enables believers to fulfill the righteous requirements of the law, not through their own strength but through the power of the Spirit working within them.

Paul speaks of this transformative power in Romans 8:3-4:

> "For God has done what the law, weakened by the flesh, could not do. By sending his own Son in the likeness of sinful flesh... in order that the righteous requirement of the law might be fulfilled in us, who walk not according to the flesh but according to the Spirit." (ESV)

The Holy Spirit enables believers to "walk according to the Spirit," meaning they live in alignment with God's will, not because they are externally compelled but because their hearts have been changed. The Spirit produces the fruit of righteousness in their lives, reflecting the internalization of God's law.

4.3 The Spirit as the Seal of the New Covenant

In addition to empowering obedience, the Holy Spirit serves as the seal and guarantee of the New Covenant. Paul describes the Holy Spirit as the "guarantee" of believers' inheritance in Christ, signifying their belonging to God and their participation in the New Covenant.

In Ephesians 1:13-14, Paul writes:

> "In him you also, when you heard the word of truth, the gospel of your salvation, and believed in him, were sealed with the promised Holy Spirit, who is the guarantee of our inheritance until we acquire possession of it." (ESV)

The Holy Spirit's presence in the life of the believer is the evidence that they are participants in the New Covenant, experiencing the forgiveness, transformation, and relationship with God that Jeremiah promised.

5. Living Under the New Covenant: The Transformed Heart

For Christians, living under the New Covenant means living in the reality of a transformed heart, empowered by the Holy Spirit to live in accordance with God's will. This transformation is not merely about outward obedience to rules but about an internal, Spirit-led relationship with God that produces a new way of living.

5.1 The Fruit of the Spirit

The evidence of the law written on the heart is seen in the transformation of character that comes through the work of the Holy Spirit. In Galatians 5:22-23, Paul describes the fruit of the Spirit:

> "But the fruit of the Spirit is love, joy, peace, patience, kindness, goodness, faithfulness, gentleness, self-control; against such things there is no law." (ESV)

These virtues are not produced by human effort but by the Spirit's work within the believer, demonstrating the internalization of God's law and the fulfillment of Jeremiah's promise.

5.2 Freedom in Christ

Living under the New Covenant also brings freedom. Unlike the Old Covenant, which required strict adherence to external regulations, the New Covenant offers believers freedom in Christ. This freedom is not a license to sin but a freedom to live in alignment with God's will, empowered by the Spirit.

In 2 Corinthians 3:17, Paul writes:

> "Now the Lord is the Spirit, and where the Spirit of the Lord is, there is freedom." (ESV)

This freedom reflects the New Covenant's emphasis on internal transformation rather than external legalism. Believers are free to live as God's people, guided by the Spirit, with His law written on their hearts.

6. Conclusion: The Law Written on Hearts Through the Holy Spirit

Jeremiah's promise of a New Covenant, where God's law would be written on the hearts of His people, finds its fulfillment in the life, death, and resurrection of Jesus Christ and the indwelling of the Holy Spirit. The Holy Spirit plays a central role in this transformation, enabling believers to live in obedience to God's will, not through external compulsion but through the internal renewal of the heart.

For Christians, the New Covenant represents a new way of relating to God, characterized by intimacy, grace, and empowerment through the Holy Spirit. The law written on the heart signifies the profound spiritual transformation that occurs under the New Covenant, allowing believers to live as God's people, with His presence dwelling within them. This fulfillment of Jeremiah's prophecy marks the beginning of a new era in the relationship between God and humanity, one that is defined by the inner work of the Holy Spirit and the transformative power of God's grace.

THE SHEPHERD-KING

1. Introduction: The Shepherd as a Biblical Metaphor

In the Bible, the metaphor of a shepherd is often used to describe the relationship between leaders and their people, with God Himself frequently being portrayed as the ultimate Shepherd of Israel. The image of a shepherd reflects both the care and responsibility that leaders have toward those they are entrusted to protect and guide. Shepherds were responsible for providing for their sheep, guiding them to safe pastures, and protecting them from predators. In the Old Testament, the leaders of Israel, especially the kings and priests, were often referred to as shepherds, tasked with leading the people in righteousness and obedience to God.

In Jeremiah 23:1-4, the prophet condemns the leaders of Israel—particularly its kings and priests—for failing in their role as shepherds. These corrupt leaders had scattered and harmed the people instead of protecting and guiding them. Jeremiah's words are a stern rebuke, but they also contain a message of hope, as God promises to gather His scattered flock and set up righteous shepherds to care for them.

This metaphor of the shepherd is particularly significant in Christian theology, where Jesus is seen as the fulfillment of the ideal Shepherd-King. In John 10:11, Jesus declares, "I am the good shepherd. The good shepherd lays down his life for the sheep" (ESV). This chapter will explore the prophetic message of Jeremiah regarding the failed shepherds of Israel, the promise of a righteous Shepherd-King, and how Jesus fulfills this role in the New Testament.

2. The Shepherds of Israel: A Message of Judgment

Throughout the book of Jeremiah, the prophet frequently addresses the failure of Israel's leaders to properly shepherd the people. These leaders, often referred to as "shepherds," included the kings, priests, and false prophets who were entrusted with the care of God's people but had led them astray. Jeremiah delivers a strong message of judgment against these corrupt leaders in Jeremiah 23:1-2:

> "Woe to the shepherds who destroy and scatter the sheep of my pasture!" declares the LORD. "Therefore thus says the LORD, the God of Israel, concerning the shepherds who care for my people: You have scattered my flock and have driven them away, and you have not attended to them. Behold, I will attend to you for your evil deeds, declares the LORD." (ESV)

2.1 The Failure of Israel's Leaders

The leaders of Israel are condemned for their failure to fulfill their duties as shepherds. Instead of guiding the people in righteousness, they had led them into idolatry, injustice, and disobedience. This failure is often seen in the kings of Judah, who ignored God's laws and allowed the people to worship false gods, as well as in the priests and prophets who preached lies and false assurances of peace. These leaders, rather than protecting the flock, had scattered them, leaving them vulnerable to destruction and exile.

In the historical context of Jeremiah's ministry, the kingdom of Judah was in decline. The people had turned away from God, and the leadership, rather than correcting their path, had only contributed to their downfall. Jeremiah often spoke against the kings and false prophets, warning them of the consequences of their disobedience. In Jeremiah 10:21, he laments:

> "For the shepherds are stupid and do not inquire of the LORD; therefore they have not prospered, and all their flock is scattered." (ESV)

The failure of the shepherds to seek God's guidance resulted in the scattering of the flock—symbolizing the spiritual and physical exile of the people of Israel.

2.2 Judgment on the Shepherds

In response to the failure of these leaders, God declares His judgment upon them. In Jeremiah 23:2, God promises to "attend to" these shepherds for their evil deeds. This judgment indicates that the leaders of Israel would be held accountable for their failure to care for God's people. The scattering of the people, which led to the Babylonian exile, was in part the result of the corruption and unfaithfulness of Israel's leaders.

The rebuke of the shepherds in Jeremiah echoes similar messages in other prophetic books. For instance, Ezekiel 34 also condemns the shepherds of Israel for neglecting the flock and taking advantage of the people for their own gain. In Ezekiel's prophecy, God also promises to remove these corrupt leaders and take on the role of the shepherd Himself.

3. The Promise of a Righteous Shepherd

While Jeremiah condemns the failed leadership of Israel, his message is not solely one of judgment. In the same passage where the false shepherds are condemned, God promises to intervene and restore His people. In Jeremiah 23:3-4, we see the promise of a future restoration and a righteous leadership:

> "Then I will gather the remnant of my flock out of all the countries where I have driven them, and I will bring them back to their fold, and they shall be fruitful and multiply. I will set shepherds over them who will care for them, and they shall fear no more, nor be dismayed, neither shall any be missing, declares the LORD." (ESV)

3.1 God Gathers the Scattered Flock

The imagery of a scattered flock is significant in this prophecy. The people of Israel, because of their disobedience and the failure of their leaders, had been scattered in exile. However, God promises to gather them again. This gathering reflects God's faithfulness to His covenant with Israel, despite their unfaithfulness. He will not abandon His people but will bring them back to their land, where they will experience renewal and prosperity.

The promise of gathering the remnant also points forward to a greater restoration. While this prophecy had an immediate fulfillment in the return of the exiles to Jerusalem after the Babylonian captivity, Christians see in it a foreshadowing of the ultimate gathering of God's people through the ministry of the Messiah, Jesus Christ.

3.2 The Appointment of Righteous Shepherds

In contrast to the corrupt shepherds who had scattered the flock, God promises to appoint shepherds who will care for the people. These shepherds will ensure that the people are no longer afraid or dismayed and that none of them will be missing. This image of the righteous shepherd reflects God's desire to provide leaders who will lead the people in righteousness, truth, and justice.

For Christians, this promise of righteous shepherds is ultimately fulfilled in Jesus Christ, the Good Shepherd, who gathers His people and cares for them in a way that no earthly leader ever could. While God may appoint faithful human leaders, the true fulfillment of this prophecy is found in Jesus, who not only leads the flock but also lays down His life for them.

4. Jesus as the Good Shepherd

The metaphor of the shepherd reaches its fullest expression in the New Testament, where Jesus identifies Himself as the Good Shepherd who gathers, protects, and sacrifices for His sheep. In John 10:11, Jesus declares:

> "I am the good shepherd. The good shepherd lays down his life for the sheep." (ESV)

This claim directly connects Jesus to the prophetic imagery found in Jeremiah and other Old Testament passages. Jesus presents Himself as the Shepherd-King who fulfills God's promise to care for His people, reversing the failures of the corrupt leaders of Israel.

4.1 Jesus Gathers His Flock

In His ministry, Jesus is depicted as gathering a scattered and lost people. He reaches out to the marginalized, the sinners, and the outcasts, bringing them into His fold. In John 10:14-16, Jesus speaks of His intimate relationship with His followers and His mission to gather more into His flock:

> "I am the good shepherd. I know my own and my own know me, just as the Father knows me and I know the Father; and I lay down my life for the sheep. And I have other sheep that are not of this fold. I must bring them also, and they will listen to my voice. So there will be one flock, one shepherd." (ESV)

Here, Jesus not only speaks of His close relationship with His followers but also hints at the inclusion of Gentiles into the flock, fulfilling the universal scope of the New Covenant. His mission as the Good Shepherd is to gather all who belong to Him, from Israel and beyond, into one united people of God.

4.2 The Sacrificial Shepherd

One of the most profound aspects of Jesus as the Good Shepherd is His willingness to lay down His life for the sheep. In contrast to the false shepherds who exploited the flock for their own gain, Jesus sacrifices Himself for the sake of His people. This self-giving love is at the heart of the Christian understanding of Jesus as the Shepherd-King.

In John 10:18, Jesus emphasizes that His sacrifice is voluntary:

> "No one takes it from me, but I lay it down of my own accord. I have authority to lay it down, and I have authority to take it up again. This charge I have received from my Father." (ESV)

Jesus' death on the cross is seen as the ultimate act of love and protection, fulfilling His role as the Good Shepherd. His sacrifice provides not only physical protection but eternal salvation for His sheep, ensuring that they will never be lost or abandoned.

4.3 Jesus the Shepherd-King

The image of Jesus as the Good Shepherd is not only one of sacrificial love but also of kingship. As the Shepherd-King, Jesus leads His people with justice, wisdom, and compassion. This echoes the prophetic promise in Jeremiah 23:5-6, where the coming King from David's line is described as a righteous Branch who will reign wisely and execute justice.

For Christians, Jesus is both the Good Shepherd who cares for the flock and the King who reigns over God's people with righteousness. His kingship is marked by humility and service, yet He also has the authority to protect, guide, and judge His people.

5. The Shepherd and the Flock in Christian Life

The role of Jesus as the Shepherd-King has deep implications for Christian life and practice. Christians understand themselves as the sheep of Jesus' flock, dependent on Him for guidance, protection, and sustenance. The relationship between Jesus and His followers is one of deep trust, as they rely on Him for both spiritual nourishment and direction.

5.1 Trusting in the Good Shepherd

Jesus' role as the Good Shepherd calls believers to place their trust in Him fully. In Psalm 23, one of the most famous passages in the Bible, the psalmist describes God as the Shepherd who leads His people beside still waters and restores their souls. For Christians, Jesus fulfills this role by providing spiritual rest and restoration through His presence and guidance.

In John 10:27-28, Jesus speaks of the security and assurance that comes from being part of His flock:

> "My sheep hear my voice, and I know them, and they follow me. I give them eternal life, and they will never perish, and no one will snatch them out of my hand." (ESV)

This promise of eternal security gives Christians confidence that, as part of Jesus' flock, they are protected and cared for, even in the face of danger and trials.

5.2 Following the Shepherd

As the Shepherd-King, Jesus calls His followers to listen to His voice and follow Him. This involves a life of discipleship, where believers seek to align their lives with Jesus' teachings and example. Just as sheep follow their shepherd, Christians are called to follow Jesus in faith, obedience, and trust.

In 1 Peter 2:25, Peter reminds believers that Jesus is the Shepherd and Overseer of their souls, and He calls them to live in light of this truth:

> "For you were straying like sheep, but have now returned to the Shepherd and Overseer of your souls." (ESV)

This return to the Shepherd marks the beginning of a new life under His care and guidance.

6. Conclusion: Jesus as the Fulfillment of the Shepherd-King

The image of the shepherd in the Bible is a powerful metaphor for leadership, care, and protection. In Jeremiah 23, the prophet condemns the false shepherds of Israel who failed to lead the people in righteousness, scattering them and leaving them vulnerable. However, God promises to gather His people and appoint a righteous Shepherd-King who will care for them faithfully.

For Christians, this prophecy finds its ultimate fulfillment in Jesus Christ, the Good Shepherd who gathers His people, sacrifices His life for them, and reigns as their eternal King. Through His ministry, death, and resurrection, Jesus fulfills the role of the Shepherd-King, providing salvation, security, and guidance for His flock. As the Good Shepherd, Jesus leads His people into a relationship of trust, care, and eternal life, fulfilling the ancient promises of God and inaugurating the new covenant with His blood.

Shepherd Imagery in Jeremiah

1. Introduction: The Symbolism of the Shepherd in Ancient Israel

In the biblical world, the image of the shepherd carried deep significance. Shepherds were responsible for leading, feeding, and protecting their sheep, and the relationship between the shepherd and the flock was one of care, guidance, and trust. This metaphor naturally extended to leadership in ancient Israel, where kings, prophets, and priests were often described as shepherds of God's people. The role of these leaders was to guide the people in righteousness, protect them from spiritual danger, and ensure their well-being.

In the Book of Jeremiah, the metaphor of the shepherd is frequently used to portray both the failure of Israel's leaders and God's promise to raise up faithful shepherds who will restore and care for His people. Jeremiah condemns the corrupt leaders of his time, using the image of failed shepherds who have led the people astray, while also pointing forward to the hope of a coming Shepherd-King who will rule with justice and righteousness. This chapter will review how shepherds are portrayed in Jeremiah's prophecies, exploring the significance of the shepherd imagery within the context of ancient Israel and its relevance in Jeremiah's message.

2. The Role of the Shepherd in Ancient Israel

To understand the prophetic use of shepherd imagery in Jeremiah, it is important to first understand the role of a shepherd in the daily life of ancient Israel. Shepherding was a common occupation in Israel, especially during the time of the patriarchs and in the early history of the nation. Shepherds were responsible for caring for their flocks, leading them to safe pastures, providing water, and protecting them from predators. This occupation required diligence, patience, and selflessness, as the well-being of the sheep depended entirely on the shepherd's attentiveness and care.

2.1 The Shepherd as a Metaphor for Leadership

Given the shepherd's role as protector and guide, it is no surprise that this image was used as a metaphor for leadership in ancient Israel. Kings, prophets, and priests were often described as shepherds of God's people, tasked with leading the nation in righteousness and ensuring the spiritual and physical welfare of the community.

In the Old Testament, the shepherd metaphor is applied to various leaders, including King David, who was originally a literal shepherd before becoming the king of Israel. David's background as a shepherd made him a fitting symbol of the ideal king, one who cares for his people as a shepherd cares for his flock. Psalm 78:70-72 reflects this metaphor:

> "He chose David his servant and took him from the sheepfolds; from following the nursing ewes he brought him to shepherd Jacob his people, Israel his inheritance. With upright heart he shepherded them and guided them with his skillful hand." (ESV)

This imagery reveals the expectation that Israel's leaders were to act as shepherds, guiding the people with wisdom, compassion, and righteousness. However, as Jeremiah reveals, the leaders of his time had failed miserably in fulfilling this role.

3. Shepherds in Jeremiah: Condemnation of Failed Leadership

Throughout the Book of Jeremiah, the prophet uses the metaphor of the shepherd to condemn the kings, priests, and false prophets of Israel for their failure to lead the people in righteousness. These leaders, tasked with guiding the nation spiritually and morally, had instead led the people into idolatry, injustice, and destruction. Jeremiah's prophetic rebukes of these leaders often use the image of the shepherd to expose their neglect and corruption.

3.1 The Shepherds Who Scatter the Flock

One of the most vivid uses of the shepherd metaphor in Jeremiah is found in Jeremiah 23:1-2, where the prophet delivers a message of judgment against the leaders of Israel:

> "Woe to the shepherds who destroy and scatter the sheep of my pasture!" declares the LORD. "Therefore thus says the LORD, the God of Israel, concerning the shepherds who care for my people: You have scattered my flock and

have driven them away, and you have not attended to them. Behold, I will attend to you for your evil deeds, declares the LORD." (ESV)

In this passage, the shepherds (Israel's leaders) are accused of scattering the flock—God's people—rather than protecting and gathering them. The failure of the leaders to care for the people had left them vulnerable to destruction and exile. Instead of leading the people toward faithfulness to God, the shepherds had driven them into idolatry, leading to national disaster.

This indictment of Israel's leaders is not just a critique of their political leadership but also their spiritual failure. The leaders had a responsibility to ensure that the people remained faithful to the covenant with God, but they had neglected this role, resulting in spiritual and physical scattering. The reference to "scattering" evokes the literal scattering of the people during the Babylonian exile, a consequence of the nation's collective failure to follow God's law.

3.2 Corrupt Shepherds and False Prophets

Jeremiah not only critiques the kings and political leaders of Israel but also the false prophets, who were supposed to provide spiritual guidance. These prophets had led the people astray by proclaiming false visions of peace and security, even as disaster loomed. In Jeremiah 14:13-14, Jeremiah denounces these false prophets:

> "Then I said: 'Ah, Lord GOD, behold, the prophets say to them, "You shall not see the sword, nor shall you have famine, but I will give you assured peace in this place."' And the LORD said to me: 'The prophets are prophesying lies in my name. I did not send them, nor did I command them or speak to them. They are prophesying to you a lying vision, worthless divination, and the deceit of their own minds.'" (ESV)

The false prophets, like corrupt shepherds, had lulled the people into complacency by assuring them that no harm would come to them, despite their rebellion against God. This deception left the people unprepared for the judgment that was coming, and it further deepened the nation's spiritual crisis. These false shepherds had failed to protect the people spiritually, leading them into false security and away from true repentance.

4. God as the True Shepherd and the Promise of Restoration

Despite the failure of Israel's human shepherds, Jeremiah's message is not without hope. God promises to take matters into His own hands, acting as the true Shepherd who will gather His people and care for them. This message of hope is found in the same passage where Jeremiah condemns the failed shepherds. In Jeremiah 23:3-4, God promises to restore His flock:

> "Then I will gather the remnant of my flock out of all the countries where I have driven them, and I will bring them back to their fold, and they shall be fruitful and multiply. I will set shepherds over them who will care for them, and they shall fear no more, nor be dismayed, neither shall any be missing, declares the LORD." (ESV)

4.1 God as the Ultimate Shepherd

In this promise of restoration, God takes on the role of the true Shepherd who will gather His scattered people. While human leaders had failed, God Himself would intervene to ensure the survival and flourishing of His flock. This image of God as the Shepherd is seen throughout the Old Testament, most famously in Psalm 23, where David declares, "The LORD is my shepherd; I shall not want."

In Jeremiah, God's role as Shepherd involves not only gathering the people back from exile but also appointing faithful shepherds who will care for them. This future vision of righteous leadership contrasts sharply with the corrupt shepherds of Jeremiah's day, and it anticipates the coming of a leader who will truly embody the qualities of a good shepherd.

4.2 The Promise of the Righteous Branch

The promise of God as the Shepherd-King who will restore His people is further developed in Jeremiah 23:5-6, where Jeremiah prophesies the coming of the Righteous Branch from the line of David:

> "Behold, the days are coming, declares the LORD, when I will raise up for David a righteous Branch, and he shall reign as king and deal wisely, and shall execute justice and righteousness in the land. In his days Judah will be saved, and Israel will dwell securely." (ESV)

This prophecy points to a future Shepherd-King who will lead the people with justice and righteousness. For Christians, this prophecy is seen as a direct reference to Jesus Christ, the ultimate Shepherd-King who fulfills the promise of gathering and caring for God's people. Jesus, referred to as the "Good Shepherd" in John 10:11, embodies the qualities of the righteous shepherd that Jeremiah foretold.

5. The Significance of the Shepherd Imagery in Jeremiah

The use of shepherd imagery in Jeremiah serves multiple purposes. It functions as a critique of failed leadership, a symbol of God's care and protection, and a promise of future restoration. The shepherd metaphor carries deep theological significance in the context of ancient Israel's covenant relationship with God and provides a powerful lens through which to understand both the failures of Israel's leaders and the hope of a future Shepherd-King.

5.1 Leadership and Responsibility

The shepherd imagery highlights the responsibility that leaders have toward their people. In ancient Israel, kings, priests, and prophets were expected to lead the nation in accordance with God's law, protecting them spiritually and ensuring their faithfulness to the covenant. When these leaders failed, the consequences were disastrous, not only for the leaders themselves but for the entire nation.

Jeremiah's use of the shepherd metaphor reinforces the idea that leadership is a sacred trust, and those who fail in their duties will be held accountable by God. The corrupt shepherds of Jeremiah's time faced God's judgment, while the promise of faithful shepherds in the future offers hope for restored leadership that will care for the people properly.

5.2 God's Faithfulness

Despite the failure of human leaders, the shepherd imagery in Jeremiah emphasizes God's faithfulness to His people. Even when the shepherds of Israel scattered the flock, God promises to gather them again and care for them Himself. This reflects God's unchanging commitment to His covenant and His people, even when they are unfaithful.

The promise of God as the ultimate Shepherd provides comfort and hope to the people of Israel during a time of great turmoil. It reassures them that, despite their current circumstances, God will not abandon them but will restore them under the leadership of a righteous Shepherd-King.

6. Conclusion: The Shepherd Metaphor as a Vision of Hope and Judgment

The shepherd imagery in Jeremiah serves as both a condemnation of the failed leadership of Israel and a hopeful promise of restoration. While the leaders of Israel had failed to guide and protect the people, scattering the flock and leading them into destruction, God promises to act as the true Shepherd who will gather His people and set over them faithful leaders. This promise finds its ultimate fulfillment in the Christian understanding of Jesus Christ as the Good Shepherd, who gathers, protects, and sacrifices for His flock.

For the people of Jeremiah's time, the shepherd metaphor was a powerful reminder of the importance of faithful leadership and the consequences of spiritual neglect. But it also pointed forward to a time of renewal and restoration, when God Himself would shepherd His people and appoint righteous leaders who would care for them with wisdom and justice. This dual message of judgment and hope continues to resonate in the Christian tradition, where Jesus is seen as the fulfillment of God's promise to be the faithful Shepherd-King.

The Corrupt Shepherds

1. Introduction: The Corrupt Shepherds of Israel

In the Book of Jeremiah, one of the recurring themes is the rebuke of the corrupt leaders, or "shepherds," of Israel. These leaders—kings, priests, and false prophets—are condemned for failing in their duties to guide, protect, and nurture God's people. Instead of leading the people in righteousness, they mislead them, allowing injustice, idolatry, and disobedience to flourish. Jeremiah's strong denunciations of these leaders highlight their role in the downfall of the nation, culminating in the Babylonian exile.

This theme of corrupt leadership is not limited to Jeremiah's time. It also finds strong parallels in the leadership during Jesus' time, particularly in the religious authorities who similarly failed to guide the people in true righteousness. Jesus, like Jeremiah, delivered a sharp rebuke to the religious leaders of His day, accusing them of hypocrisy, greed, and spiritual blindness. In this chapter, we will explore the corrupt shepherds that Jeremiah condemned and examine how his rebuke parallels Jesus' critique of the religious leaders in the Gospels.

2. Jeremiah's Rebuke of the Corrupt Shepherds

Jeremiah's critique of Israel's leadership is rooted in the metaphor of the shepherd—a term used throughout Scripture to describe those entrusted with the care of God's people. The leaders of Israel, symbolized as shepherds, were supposed to protect, nurture, and guide the nation in faithfulness to God's covenant. However, during Jeremiah's time, these leaders had become corrupt, self-serving, and neglectful.

2.1 The Scattering of the Flock

In Jeremiah 23:1-2, the prophet delivers a harsh message of judgment against the leaders, accusing them of scattering the people rather than gathering them:

> "Woe to the shepherds who destroy and scatter the sheep of my pasture!" declares the LORD. "Therefore thus says the LORD, the God of Israel, concerning the shepherds who care for my people: You have scattered my flock and have driven them away, and you have not attended to them. Behold, I will attend to you for your evil deeds, declares the LORD." (ESV)

These leaders are charged with driving the people away from God rather than leading them in obedience to His laws. Instead of protecting the flock, they have allowed the people to become vulnerable, spiritually lost, and open to destruction. The failure to attend to the spiritual and physical needs of the people resulted in their exile and suffering.

2.2 Leading the People into Idolatry

A significant part of the corruption among Israel's leaders was their encouragement, or at least their tolerance, of idolatry. The kings, priests, and false prophets permitted and even promoted the worship of foreign gods, leading the people into spiritual apostasy. This disobedience to the covenant had catastrophic consequences, as the leaders failed to uphold their responsibility to ensure the nation's exclusive worship of Yahweh.

In Jeremiah 10:21, the prophet denounces the shepherds for their lack of understanding:

> "For the shepherds are stupid and do not inquire of the LORD; therefore they have not prospered, and all their flock is scattered." (ESV)

By neglecting to seek God's wisdom and allowing the people to engage in idolatry, the leaders had brought disaster upon the nation. Their failure to uphold the covenant with God was directly responsible for the scattering of the people in exile.

2.3 The Selfishness of the Shepherds

Jeremiah also critiques the selfishness of the leaders, who sought their own gain at the expense of the people.

Instead of serving the flock, these leaders exploited them, using their positions for personal enrichment. In Jeremiah 6:13, the prophet condemns both priests and prophets for their greed:

> "For from the least to the greatest of them, everyone is greedy for unjust gain; and from prophet to priest, everyone deals falsely." (ESV)

The leaders' pursuit of wealth and power had corrupted their ability to lead the people in righteousness. Their false assurances of peace and security, given in exchange for material gain, left the people unprepared for the coming judgment and exile.

3. Parallels in Jesus' Rebuke of the Religious Leaders

Just as Jeremiah condemned the corrupt shepherds of his day, Jesus, centuries later, delivered a scathing critique of the religious leaders of Israel. In the Gospels, Jesus rebukes the Pharisees, scribes, and other religious authorities for their hypocrisy, greed, and failure to truly lead the people in the ways of God. The parallels between Jeremiah's rebuke and Jesus' critique reveal a recurring theme of failed leadership in Israel's history.

3.1 The Hypocrisy of the Pharisees

One of Jesus' strongest criticisms of the religious leaders in His time was their hypocrisy. The Pharisees, who were the religious elite, prided themselves on strict adherence to the Mosaic Law, yet their outward religiosity masked inward corruption. They emphasized ritual purity, tithing, and public displays of piety, but neglected the deeper matters of justice, mercy, and faithfulness.

In Matthew 23:23, Jesus rebukes the Pharisees for their misplaced priorities:

> "Woe to you, scribes and Pharisees, hypocrites! For you tithe mint and dill and cumin, and have neglected the weightier matters of the law: justice and mercy and faithfulness. These you ought to have done, without neglecting the others." (ESV)

Like the corrupt shepherds of Jeremiah's day, the Pharisees were more concerned with external appearances and maintaining their own power than with leading the people toward genuine righteousness. Their failure to embody the spirit of the law mirrored the failures of the leaders in Jeremiah's time, who neglected the true care of the flock.

3.2 Leading the People Astray

Just as Jeremiah condemned the leaders for scattering the people and leading them into idolatry, Jesus accused the religious leaders of leading the people astray through their false teachings and legalistic burdens. The Pharisees imposed heavy religious demands on the people, creating barriers between them and God's grace.

In Matthew 23:13, Jesus issues a warning to the Pharisees:

> "But woe to you, scribes and Pharisees, hypocrites! For you shut the kingdom of heaven in people's faces. For you neither enter yourselves nor allow those who would enter to go in." (ESV)

By adding layers of legalistic requirements to the law, the religious leaders had made it difficult for the people to experience God's grace and forgiveness. Their teachings had become a burden, preventing the people from fully understanding or accessing the kingdom of God. This failure to guide the people into a true relationship with God parallels the spiritual neglect seen in Jeremiah's time, where the leaders allowed the people to stray into idolatry and disobedience.

3.3 Selfishness and Greed Among the Leaders

Like Jeremiah, Jesus condemned the religious leaders for their greed and exploitation of the people. The Pharisees and other leaders were often more concerned with their own wealth and status than with the well-being of the people they were supposed to serve. In Luke 20:46-47, Jesus warns His followers to beware of the self-serving scribes:

> "Beware of the scribes, who like to walk around in long robes, and love greetings in the marketplaces and the best seats in the synagogues and the places of honor at feasts, who devour widows' houses and for a pretense make long prayers. They will receive the greater condemnation." (ESV)

The religious leaders used their positions to enrich themselves at the expense of the vulnerable, much like the leaders in Jeremiah's time who sought unjust gain and dealt falsely with the people. This exploitation was a betrayal of their sacred duty to shepherd God's people with compassion and justice.

4. The Consequences of Failed Leadership: Judgment and Exile

Both Jeremiah and Jesus warned of the dire consequences that would result from the failure of Israel's leaders. In Jeremiah's time, the failure of the shepherds to lead the people in righteousness and covenant faithfulness resulted in the destruction of Jerusalem and the Babylonian exile. The scattering of the people was the ultimate consequence of the leaders' neglect and corruption.

Similarly, Jesus warned the religious leaders of His day that their hypocrisy and failure to lead the people would result in judgment. In Matthew 23:37-38, Jesus laments over Jerusalem and prophesies its destruction:

> "O Jerusalem, Jerusalem, the city that kills the prophets and stones those who are sent to it! How often would I have gathered your children together as a hen gathers her brood under her wings, and you were not willing! See, your house is left to you desolate." (ESV)

This prophecy was fulfilled in A.D. 70, when the Romans destroyed Jerusalem and the Temple, scattering the Jewish people. Just as the leaders in Jeremiah's time were held responsible for the exile, so too were the religious leaders of Jesus' time held accountable for their failure to lead the people in true faithfulness to God.

5. The Hope of a Righteous Shepherd

Despite the failures of Israel's leaders, both Jeremiah and Jesus offered hope for the future. In Jeremiah 23:5-6, the prophet points forward to the coming of a Righteous Branch from the line of David—a future Shepherd-King who would lead the people in righteousness and justice:

> "Behold, the days are coming, declares the LORD, when I will raise up for David a righteous Branch, and he shall reign as king and deal wisely, and shall execute justice and righteousness in the land. In his days Judah will be saved, and Israel will dwell securely." (ESV)

For Christians, this prophecy is fulfilled in Jesus Christ, who is seen as the ultimate Good Shepherd. In John

10:11, Jesus identifies Himself as the Good Shepherd who lays down His life for the sheep. Unlike the corrupt leaders who scattered the flock, Jesus gathers His people, offering them eternal life and protection.

The promise of a righteous Shepherd-King offers hope in the face of failed leadership, reminding the people of God's faithfulness and His plan to restore His flock through the leadership of the Messiah.

6. Conclusion: Corrupt Shepherds and the Hope of Restoration

Jeremiah's rebuke of the corrupt leaders of Israel mirrors the sharp critique that Jesus delivered against the religious leaders of His day. Both prophets condemned the leaders for their hypocrisy, greed, and failure to properly guide God's people. The consequences of their neglect were dire, leading to exile in Jeremiah's time and the destruction of Jerusalem in Jesus' time.

However, in both cases, there is also a message of hope. Jeremiah prophesied the coming of a righteous Shepherd-King who would restore the people and lead them in justice and righteousness. Christians believe this prophecy is fulfilled in Jesus Christ, who as the Good Shepherd gathers His people and provides for their eternal security.

The corrupt shepherds may have failed, but the promise of a faithful Shepherd offers a vision of restoration and hope, reminding believers that God remains committed to His people, even when human leaders fall short.

Jesus as the Good Shepherd

1. Introduction: The Shepherd-King and Its Fulfillment in Jesus

The image of the shepherd is deeply rooted in biblical tradition, symbolizing leadership, care, and responsibility. In the Old Testament, God frequently refers to the leaders of Israel—particularly kings, priests, and prophets—as shepherds who are entrusted with the care of His people. This metaphor also carries significant weight when God is referred to as the ultimate Shepherd of His people, providing protection, guidance, and provision.

In the Book of Jeremiah, the prophet speaks of corrupt shepherds who have failed to lead the people of Israel in righteousness, but he also offers a promise of a future Righteous Shepherd-King who will gather and protect God's flock. For Christians, this prophecy finds its ultimate fulfillment in the person of Jesus Christ, who, in the New Testament, is referred to as the Good Shepherd. Through His life, teachings, sacrificial death, and resurrection, Jesus perfectly fulfills the role of the Shepherd-King, embodying the care, justice, and leadership that Israel's leaders had failed to provide.

In this chapter, we will explore how Jesus fulfills the role of the Good Shepherd, examining the connections between the Old Testament prophecies and the New Testament portrayal of Jesus, as well as the significance of His shepherding role for Christian theology.

2. The Prophecy of a Righteous Shepherd in the Old Testament

Throughout the Old Testament, the metaphor of a shepherd is used to describe both God's relationship with His people and the responsibilities of Israel's leaders. When the leaders failed, God often spoke of taking on the role of the shepherd Himself or raising up a faithful leader who would fulfill the shepherding role.

2.1 Failed Shepherds and the Promise of a Righteous Branch

As discussed earlier, Jeremiah 23:1-4 condemns the corrupt shepherds of Israel who had scattered and destroyed the flock. But God promises that He will intervene to restore His people and appoint righteous shepherds to care for them. This leads into the prophecy of the Righteous Branch from the line of David, found in Jeremiah 23:5-6:

> "Behold, the days are coming, declares the Lord, when I will raise up for David a righteous Branch, and He shall reign as king and deal wisely, and shall execute justice and righteousness in the land. In His days Judah will be saved, and Israel will dwell securely. And this is the name by which He will be called: 'The Lord is our righteousness.'" (ESV)

The promise of a righteous ruler who will reign with justice and wisdom is directly connected to the image of a good and faithful shepherd. This prophecy offers hope for a leader who will not only restore the nation physically but will also lead them into a right relationship with God.

2.2 The Good Shepherd in Ezekiel

In addition to Jeremiah, the prophet Ezekiel also uses the shepherd metaphor to condemn Israel's leaders and to promise a future shepherd. In Ezekiel 34:11-16, God declares that He Himself will search for His sheep and gather them:

> "For thus says the Lord God: Behold, I, I myself will search for my sheep and will seek them out... I will rescue them from all places where they have been scattered on a day of clouds and thick darkness." (ESV)

God promises to gather His people like a shepherd gathers his flock, providing for their needs and protecting them. Later in the same chapter, God promises to raise up one shepherd over them—"my servant David"—who will tend them and be their shepherd. This is a messianic prophecy that Christians believe points to Jesus as the fulfillment of the Davidic shepherd-king.

3. Jesus Declares Himself as the Good Shepherd

The fulfillment of the Shepherd-King prophecies in the Old Testament is most clearly seen in the teachings of Jesus, particularly in John 10, where Jesus explicitly refers to Himself as the Good Shepherd. In this passage, Jesus explains His unique role in caring for and protecting His people, in contrast to the false and corrupt shepherds who neglect their duties.

3.1 The Good Shepherd Who Lays Down His Life

In John 10:11, Jesus makes a profound declaration:

> "I am the good shepherd. The good shepherd lays down his life for the sheep." (ESV)

This statement not only identifies Jesus as the Good Shepherd prophesied in the Old Testament but also reveals the nature of His shepherding. Unlike the corrupt leaders who exploited the people for their own gain, Jesus defines His leadership through sacrificial love. He willingly lays down His life to protect and save His flock—a reference to His impending death on the cross. This self-sacrificial act is the ultimate expression of a shepherd's care, fulfilling the role of the Shepherd-King in a way that no earthly leader could.

The sacrificial aspect of Jesus' shepherding contrasts with the "hired hand" that He describes in John 10:12-13, who abandons the sheep when danger arises. Jesus is the true Shepherd who remains with His sheep even in the face of danger, laying down His life to protect them from the ultimate threat of sin and death.

3.2 The Intimacy Between the Shepherd and His Sheep

Another key aspect of Jesus' role as the Good Shepherd is the intimate relationship He has with His followers. In John 10:14-15, Jesus speaks of the deep knowledge and connection between Himself and His sheep:

> "I am the good shepherd. I know my own and my own know me, just as the Father knows me and I know the Father; and I lay down my life for the sheep." (ESV)

This intimate knowledge mirrors the relationship between Jesus and the Father, emphasizing the depth of His care for each member of His flock. This image reflects the personal relationship that Jesus offers to His followers, one in which they are known, loved, and cared for individually.

In contrast to the impersonal and negligent leadership of the corrupt shepherds, Jesus' shepherding is marked by relational closeness and commitment. The sheep recognize

His voice and follow Him, trusting in His guidance and protection.

3.3 The Gathering of the Scattered Flock

Jesus also speaks of gathering other sheep who are not of the same fold, indicating the universal scope of His mission. In John 10:16, He says:

> "And I have other sheep that are not of this fold. I must bring them also, and they will listen to my voice. So there will be one flock, one shepherd." (ESV)

This reference is often understood as Jesus' mission to gather both Jews and Gentiles into one unified flock under His care. In this way, Jesus fulfills the prophecies of the Old Testament, where God promises to gather His scattered people. His mission extends beyond Israel to include all who would follow Him, fulfilling the vision of a Shepherd-King who reigns over all nations and peoples.

4. Jesus as the Fulfillment of the Shepherd-King Role

Jesus' identification as the Good Shepherd in John 10 is not an isolated teaching but is deeply connected to the broader biblical theme of the Shepherd-King. By fulfilling the role of the Good Shepherd, Jesus completes the Old Testament prophecies that spoke of a righteous and faithful leader who would gather, protect, and lead God's people.

4.1 The Shepherd-King Who Gathers His People

Throughout the Gospels, Jesus is depicted as fulfilling the role of the Shepherd-King by gathering the lost, the outcasts, and the marginalized. He actively seeks out those who are spiritually lost, much like a shepherd searching for a lost sheep. This is vividly illustrated in the parable of the lost sheep in Luke 15:4-7, where Jesus compares Himself to a shepherd who leaves the ninety-nine sheep to search for the one that is lost, rejoicing when it is found.

This act of gathering the lost reflects Jesus' fulfillment of God's promise to regather His people. Jesus, as the Shepherd-King, restores the scattered flock of Israel and expands His mission to include the Gentiles, bringing all believers under His care as one unified people.

4.2 The Shepherd-King Who Protects and Provides

As the Good Shepherd, Jesus not only gathers but also protects and provides for His people. In John 10:9, Jesus offers the promise of abundant life:

> "I am the door. If anyone enters by me, he will be saved and will go in and out and find pasture." (ESV)

Jesus protects His flock from spiritual danger, offering salvation and eternal life. In the same way that a shepherd leads his sheep to safe pastures, Jesus leads His followers to spiritual nourishment and security. His death and resurrection provide ultimate protection from the consequences of sin and death, ensuring that those who follow Him will never be snatched from His hand (John 10:28-29).

4.3 The Shepherd-King Who Reigns with Justice and Righteousness

Jesus' role as the Shepherd-King is also characterized by His just and righteous reign. In contrast to the corrupt leaders condemned by Jeremiah, Jesus leads with perfect wisdom and justice. His teachings throughout the Gospels emphasize God's kingdom of righteousness, where the poor, the meek, and the peacemakers are blessed, and where love, mercy, and justice are paramount.

In the final judgment scene of Matthew 25:31-46, Jesus is depicted as the King who separates the sheep from the goats, rewarding those who have lived in accordance with His righteous kingdom. This image of Jesus as the Shepherd-King who judges with justice aligns with the prophecies of Jeremiah and Ezekiel, where the future shepherd is described as one who will execute justice and righteousness in the land.

5. The Significance of Jesus as the Good Shepherd for Christian Life

The image of Jesus as the Good Shepherd has profound implications for Christian life and theology. For Christians, Jesus' role as the Good Shepherd signifies His ongoing care, protection, and guidance in their daily lives. His willingness to lay down His life for the sheep is seen as the ultimate expression of love, and His intimate knowledge of each believer speaks to the personal nature of the Christian faith.

5.1 Trust in the Good Shepherd

One of the central themes of Jesus' teaching as the Good Shepherd is the call for His followers to trust in Him completely. Just as sheep rely on their shepherd for protection and provision, Christians are called to trust in Jesus' care and leadership. This trust is rooted in the assurance that Jesus knows His followers intimately and will never abandon them.

In Psalm 23, one of the most beloved passages in Scripture, the psalmist describes God as the Shepherd who provides, leads, and protects His people. For Christians, Jesus fulfills this role, leading them beside still waters, restoring their souls, and guiding them in paths of righteousness.

5.2 Following the Voice of the Shepherd

As the Good Shepherd, Jesus calls His followers to listen to His voice and follow Him. In John 10:27, He says:

> "My sheep hear my voice, and I know them, and they follow me." (ESV)

This call to follow Jesus is at the heart of Christian discipleship. It involves recognizing Jesus' voice through His teachings and allowing His guidance to shape one's life. In a world filled with competing voices and distractions, following the Good Shepherd requires discernment, obedience, and trust in His leadership.

6. Conclusion: Jesus as the Fulfillment of the Shepherd-King

The role of the shepherd in the Bible is one of deep care, protection, and leadership. In the Old Testament, God promised to raise up a righteous Shepherd-King who would gather, protect, and lead His people in justice and righteousness. Jesus, as the Good Shepherd, perfectly fulfills this role. Through His sacrificial death, intimate relationship with His followers, and just reign, Jesus embodies the qualities of the true Shepherd-King who offers eternal life and security to His flock.

For Christians, Jesus' role as the Good Shepherd is not only a fulfillment of ancient prophecies but also a source of ongoing comfort and guidance. He is the Shepherd who knows His sheep by name, who lays down His life for them, and who leads them into abundant life. As the Good Shepherd, Jesus continues to care for His people, providing the ultimate example of self-giving love and faithful leadership.

CHAPTER 05

SUFFERING, JUDGMENT, AND REDEMPTION

1. Introduction: The Cycle of Judgment and Redemption in Jeremiah

The Book of Jeremiah, often called a book of doom, is filled with prophecies of judgment that reflect the spiritual and moral failures of the people of Israel and their leaders. Throughout his ministry, Jeremiah warned of the coming destruction due to the nation's persistent sin, disobedience, and idolatry. Yet, alongside the harsh messages of judgment, there are also powerful promises of hope, redemption, and restoration. Jeremiah speaks of a future where God will gather

His scattered people, forgive their sins, and restore them to their land.

Christians believe that these themes of suffering, judgment, and redemption echo profoundly in the life and ministry of Jesus Christ. Jesus took on the sins of humanity, faced divine judgment through His suffering on the cross, and ultimately brought about redemption and restoration. In this chapter, we will explore how the themes of suffering, judgment, and redemption in Jeremiah are fulfilled in the life, death, and resurrection of Jesus.

2. Judgment in Jeremiah: The Consequences of Sin

Jeremiah's prophecies frequently center on the theme of judgment, which is portrayed as the inevitable consequence of Israel's disobedience. The people of Judah had turned away from God, embracing idolatry and injustice. This spiritual rebellion could not go unanswered, and Jeremiah was tasked with delivering the message that judgment was imminent.

2.1 The People's Sin and Idolatry

One of the central reasons for the coming judgment was the people's idolatry. Despite being chosen as God's covenant people, Israel repeatedly broke the covenant by worshipping foreign gods and abandoning the commandments. Jeremiah vividly describes the betrayal of the people in Jeremiah 2:13:

> "For my people have committed two evils: they have forsaken me, the fountain of living waters, and hewed out cisterns for themselves, broken cisterns that can hold no water." (ESV)

This metaphor highlights the people's abandonment of God, the source of life and sustenance, in favor of false gods who could not provide for them.

2.2 The Inevitability of Judgment

Jeremiah warned that because of this rebellion, judgment in the form of exile and destruction was inevitable. The Babylonian conquest of Judah and the destruction of Jerusalem would be the direct result of the people's unrepentant sin. In Jeremiah 25:8-9, God declares:

> "Therefore thus says the Lord of hosts: Because you have not obeyed my words, behold, I will send for all the tribes of the north, declares the Lord, and for Nebuchadnezzar the king of Babylon, my servant, and I will bring them against this land and its inhabitants." (ESV)

The Babylonians are depicted as God's instrument of judgment, and the exile represents a profound moment of divine reckoning for Judah's unfaithfulness. This judgment reflects the biblical principle that sin brings about consequences, both spiritually and physically.

3. The Promise of Redemption in Jeremiah

Even as Jeremiah delivers bleak prophecies of destruction and exile, he also speaks of God's enduring faithfulness and the promise of redemption. Jeremiah's message is not one of despair but of hope for the future, where God will gather His people, restore them, and establish a new covenant relationship.

3.1 The Promise of Restoration

One of the most significant aspects of Jeremiah's prophecies is the promise that God will restore His people after judgment. In Jeremiah 30:3, God reassures the people:

> "For behold, days are coming, declares the Lord, when I will restore the fortunes of my people, Israel and Judah, says the Lord, and I will bring them back to the land that I gave to their fathers, and they shall take possession of it." (ESV)

This promise of restoration emphasizes that while God's judgment is real, it is not the final word. God's purpose in judgment is not to destroy but to purify and renew His people. The exile, painful though it is, will eventually give way to a new beginning.

3.2 The New Covenant

Jeremiah's prophecy of the New Covenant in Jeremiah 31:31-34 is perhaps the most powerful expression of hope and redemption in the book. God promises to establish a new kind of covenant with His people, one that is internal and transformative:

> "For this is the covenant that I will make with the house of Israel after those days, declares the Lord: I will put my law within them, and I will write it on their hearts. And I will be their God, and they shall be my people." (ESV)

This New Covenant will bring about a deep, personal relationship between God and His people, marked by forgiveness and an intimate knowledge of God's will. This promise of redemption looks beyond the immediate judgment to a future where God's people are transformed and fully restored to fellowship with Him.

4. Suffering, Judgment, and Redemption in the Life of Jesus

For Christians, the themes of suffering, judgment, and redemption that permeate Jeremiah's prophecies find their ultimate fulfillment in the life, death, and resurrection of Jesus Christ. Jesus, like the people of Judah, faced suffering and judgment. However, rather than suffering for His own sins, Jesus took on the sins of the world, enduring judgment on behalf of humanity to bring about redemption.

4.1 Jesus' Suffering: The Innocent Lamb

Throughout the Gospels, Jesus' suffering is depicted as a central aspect of His mission. He endured rejection, betrayal, and ultimately crucifixion, despite His innocence. In Isaiah 53:3-5, the suffering of the Messiah is prophesied, describing Him as a man of sorrows:

> "He was despised and rejected by men; a man of sorrows, and acquainted with grief... But he was pierced for our transgressions; he was crushed for our iniquities; upon him was the chastisement that brought us peace, and with his wounds we are healed." (ESV)

This passage, which Christians see as a prophecy of Jesus' suffering, reveals that His pain was not for His own wrongdoing but for the sins of others. Jesus willingly took upon Himself the suffering that humanity deserved as the ultimate act of love and sacrifice.

4.2 Jesus' Judgment: Bearing the Sin of the World

In Christian theology, Jesus' suffering culminates in His death on the cross, where He bore the full weight of divine judgment for sin. As Jeremiah warned of the impending judgment on Judah for their sins, the New Testament reveals that Jesus faced God's judgment in place of all humanity. In 2 Corinthians 5:21, Paul explains:

> "For our sake he made him to be sin who knew no sin, so that in him we might become the righteousness of God." (ESV)

On the cross, Jesus took upon Himself the sins of the world, enduring the punishment that was rightfully due to humanity. This act of substitutionary atonement is central to Christian understanding of Jesus' mission: He was judged so that others might be redeemed.

4.3 Jesus' Redemption: Bringing New Life

The suffering and judgment that Jesus endured did not end in defeat. Through His resurrection, Jesus brought about redemption, offering new life to all who believe in Him. His resurrection represents the ultimate victory over sin and death, fulfilling the promise of restoration that Jeremiah prophesied.

In Romans 6:4, Paul connects Jesus' resurrection to the new life that believers receive:

> "We were buried therefore with him by baptism into death, in order that, just as Christ was raised from the dead by the glory of the Father, we too might walk in newness of life." (ESV)

Just as Jeremiah promised that God would restore His people and bring them back to their land, Jesus' resurrection brings about the restoration of humanity's relationship with God. Through His redemptive work, Jesus inaugurates the New Covenant that Jeremiah prophesied, where God's law is written on the hearts of believers and their sins are forgiven.

5. The Christian Understanding of Suffering, Judgment, and Redemption

For Christians, the themes of suffering, judgment, and redemption in Jeremiah resonate deeply with their understanding of Jesus' work. Jeremiah's prophecies illustrate the pattern of human sin, divine judgment, and eventual restoration—a pattern that Christians believe reaches its climax in the life, death, and resurrection of Jesus.

5.1 Suffering as a Path to Redemption

Jesus' suffering is seen not as a defeat but as a necessary path to redemption. Just as the exile was a painful but purifying experience for the people of Judah, Jesus' suffering on the cross brought about spiritual purification and redemption for all who place their faith in Him. For Christians, suffering, when united with Christ, can have redemptive value, leading to spiritual growth and transformation.

5.2 Judgment as a Means of Mercy

While Jeremiah's message of judgment was severe, it was also a call to repentance. In the same way, Jesus' death on the cross represents both judgment and mercy. Through His death, the judgment for sin is satisfied, but His sacrifice also opens the door for God's mercy and forgiveness. Christians believe that in Jesus, judgment is transformed into grace, allowing humanity to be reconciled with God.

5.3 Redemption as Restoration and New Creation

Just as Jeremiah prophesied the restoration of Israel after the exile, Christians believe that Jesus' resurrection is the ultimate act of restoration. Through Him, believers are not only forgiven but also transformed, becoming part of God's new creation. The New Covenant, established through Jesus' blood, brings about a new relationship with God, where His law is written on the hearts of believers and they are empowered to live in accordance with His will.

6. Conclusion: The Fulfillment of Jeremiah's Themes in Jesus

Jeremiah's prophecies of suffering, judgment, and redemption find their ultimate fulfillment in the life and work of Jesus Christ. Just as the people of Judah experienced the consequences of their sin and the hope of restoration, so too did Jesus take on the suffering and judgment of sin to bring about the ultimate redemption of humanity. His death and resurrection fulfilled the promise of the New Covenant, providing forgiveness, new life, and a restored relationship with God.

For Christians, the parallels between Jeremiah's prophecies and Jesus' mission serve as a powerful reminder of God's faithfulness, justice, and mercy. Though judgment is real and sin has consequences, God's desire is always for redemption and restoration. In Jesus, the hope of Jeremiah's prophecies is fully realized, offering a path to new life and eternal relationship with God.

Judgment in Jeremiah

1. Introduction: The Theme of Divine Judgment in Jeremiah

The Book of Jeremiah is marked by an overarching theme of divine judgment, directed primarily at the kingdom of Judah for its persistent rebellion against God. Jeremiah, often called the "weeping prophet," was commissioned by God to deliver a message of impending doom, warning the people of Judah of the consequences of their sin, disobedience, and idolatry. His prophecies unfolded against the backdrop of an impending Babylonian invasion that would culminate in the destruction of Jerusalem and the exile of the people.

Jeremiah's message of judgment was not arbitrary or unjust; it was a direct response to the spiritual, social, and moral failures of Judah. This chapter will explore the reasons for Judah's judgment and exile as laid out in Jeremiah, focusing on the primary sins that led to their downfall and the divine justice that underpins Jeremiah's prophecies.

2. The Covenant Relationship: Judah's Responsibility

To understand the judgment prophesied in Jeremiah, we must first recognize the covenant relationship between God and the people of Israel. This covenant, established at Mount Sinai, was a binding agreement in which God promised to bless Israel and make them His chosen people, while the Israelites were required to obey God's commandments and remain faithful to Him.

In Exodus 19:5-6, God set the terms of this covenant:

> "Now therefore, if you will indeed obey my voice and keep my covenant, you shall be my treasured possession among all peoples, for all the earth is mine; and you shall be to me a kingdom of priests and a holy nation." (ESV)

This covenant relationship shaped the identity of the people of Israel, and their fidelity to God was essential for their continued blessing and protection. However, as Jeremiah's prophecies reveal, Judah had repeatedly violated this covenant, leading to God's judgment.

3. The Primary Sins of Judah Leading to Judgment

Throughout the Book of Jeremiah, the prophet repeatedly outlines the specific sins of Judah that incurred divine wrath and led to their exile. These sins included idolatry, social injustice, rejection of God's law, and unfaithfulness to the covenant. Each of these factors played a crucial role in provoking God's judgment.

3.1 Idolatry: The Betrayal of God

One of the central reasons for Judah's judgment was its rampant idolatry. Despite God's command to worship Him alone, the people of Judah had turned to the worship of foreign gods and idols, forsaking their covenant with the Lord. Jeremiah frequently condemns the people for this spiritual adultery, describing their idolatry as a betrayal of their relationship with God.

In Jeremiah 2:11-13, the prophet vividly portrays this betrayal:

> "Has a nation changed its gods, even though they are no gods? But my people have changed their glory for that which does not profit. Be appalled, O heavens, at this; be shocked, be utterly desolate, declares the Lord, for my people have committed two evils: they have forsaken me, the fountain of living waters, and hewed out cisterns for themselves, broken cisterns that can hold no water." (ESV)

This passage highlights how the people abandoned the true source of life—God—for worthless idols, symbolized by the broken cisterns. Their pursuit of foreign gods was an act of spiritual infidelity, leading them away from the protection and blessings of their covenant with God.

Jeremiah also condemns the worship of Baal and other foreign gods, practices that often involved immoral and destructive rituals, including child sacrifice. In Jeremiah 7:9-10, God rebukes the people for their false worship:

> "Will you steal, murder, commit adultery, swear falsely, make offerings to Baal, and go after other gods that you have not known, and then come and stand before me in this house, which is called by my name, and say, 'We are delivered!'—only to go on doing all these abominations?" (ESV)

The hypocrisy of worshiping false gods while still claiming the blessings of the Lord's temple underscores the depth of Judah's spiritual corruption.

3.2 Social Injustice: The Neglect of the Vulnerable

In addition to idolatry, Judah was condemned for its rampant social injustice. Jeremiah consistently rebukes the people for exploiting the poor, neglecting the vulnerable, and allowing injustice to pervade their society. In ancient Israel, the covenant not only required faithfulness in worship but also demanded justice, mercy, and care for the marginalized.

In Jeremiah 5:26-28, the prophet describes the moral decay of Judah's leaders:

> "For wicked men are found among my people; they lurk like fowlers lying in wait. They set a trap; they catch men.

Like a cage full of birds, their houses are full of deceit; therefore they have become great and rich; they have grown fat and sleek. They know no bounds in deeds of evil; they judge not with justice the cause of the fatherless, to make it prosper, and they do not defend the rights of the needy." (ESV)

This condemnation of Judah's leaders reflects the deep corruption in society, where the powerful oppressed the weak and the vulnerable, contrary to God's command to seek justice and defend the rights of the poor. Jeremiah's message highlights that divine judgment is not only about spiritual unfaithfulness but also about the failure to uphold social righteousness.

3.3 Rejection of God's Word and Prophets

Another reason for Judah's judgment was their rejection of God's word and their unwillingness to listen to the prophets, including Jeremiah. Throughout his ministry, Jeremiah called the people to repentance, urging them to turn back to God and avoid the impending disaster. However, instead of heeding his warnings, the people mocked and persecuted him, choosing to listen to false prophets who assured them of peace and security.

In Jeremiah 6:16-17, God laments the people's stubborn refusal to listen:

> "Thus says the Lord: 'Stand by the roads, and look, and ask for the ancient paths, where the good way is; and walk in it, and find rest for your souls. But they said, 'We will not walk in it.' I set watchmen over you, saying, 'Pay attention to the sound of the trumpet!' But they said, 'We will not pay attention.'" (ESV)

The people's rejection of the true prophets and their preference for the false assurances of peace contributed to their downfall. This refusal to listen to God's word is seen as a hardened rebellion, making judgment unavoidable.

3.4 Covenant Unfaithfulness

All of Judah's sins—idolatry, social injustice, and rejection of God's prophets—culminated in a profound breach of the covenant relationship between God and His people. Throughout Jeremiah, the prophet uses the imagery of marriage to describe this broken relationship, portraying Judah as an unfaithful wife who has betrayed her covenant with her husband, God.

In Jeremiah 3:20, God expresses His heartbreak over Judah's infidelity:

> "Surely, as a treacherous wife leaves her husband, so have you been treacherous to me, O house of Israel, declares the Lord." (ESV)

This betrayal of the covenant relationship lies at the heart of Judah's judgment. The people's unfaithfulness was not simply a violation of laws but a deep rupture in their relationship with the God who had chosen and redeemed them.

4. The Nature of God's Judgment: Justice and Mercy

Jeremiah's message of judgment reveals much about the nature of God's justice. God's judgment on Judah is not arbitrary or vindictive; it is the just consequence of their persistent rebellion. However, even in His judgment, God's ultimate desire is for repentance and restoration.

4.1 The Necessity of Judgment

Judah's judgment was inevitable because God is a God of justice who cannot ignore sin and rebellion. The exile was the fulfillment of the covenant curses outlined in Deuteronomy 28, where God warned the people of the consequences of forsaking the covenant. In Jeremiah 11:10-11, God reminds the people that their actions have brought about the promised judgment:

> "They have turned back to the iniquities of their forefathers, who refused to hear my words. They have gone after other gods to serve them. The house of Israel and the house of Judah have broken my covenant that I made with

their fathers. Therefore, thus says the Lord, Behold, I am bringing disaster upon them that they cannot escape." (ESV)

God's judgment on Judah reflects His commitment to justice and His righteousness in upholding the terms of the covenant.

4.2 The Mercy Within Judgment

Even in the midst of judgment, Jeremiah's prophecies reveal God's enduring mercy. God does not delight in judgment but desires repentance and restoration. In Jeremiah 18:7-8, God explains that judgment is always conditional, dependent on the people's response:

> "If at any time I declare concerning a nation or a kingdom, that I will pluck up and break down and destroy it, and if that nation, concerning which I have spoken, turns from its evil, I will relent of the disaster that I intended to do to it." (ESV)

This passage highlights God's willingness to withhold judgment if the people repent. Despite the severity of Jeremiah's warnings, God's ultimate desire is for His people to return to Him and avoid the consequences of their sin. However, when repentance does not occur, judgment becomes a necessary act of divine justice.

The Judgment of Judah as a Call to Repentance

The judgment of Judah as prophesied in Jeremiah serves as a profound lesson about the consequences of sin, rebellion, and covenant unfaithfulness. The people's idolatry, social injustice, and rejection of God's word led to their exile and suffering. Yet, even in the midst of judgment, God's mercy shines through, offering hope for restoration and redemption.

For Christians, the judgment of Judah also serves as a reminder of the seriousness of sin and the need for repentance. Just as God judged Judah for their rebellion, He continues to call people to turn from sin and return to a relationship with Him. Jeremiah's message of judgment is ultimately one of hope, pointing to the possibility of redemption and renewal through repentance and a restored relationship with God.

The exile of Judah underscores the reality of divine justice but also reflects the enduring mercy of a God who desires to restore and redeem His people.

Jesus and Judgment

1. Introduction: Jesus as the Bearer of Judgment

In Christian theology, Jesus Christ plays a central role in bearing the judgment for humanity's sin. The judgment that was due to all people because of their disobedience to God was taken upon Jesus through His sacrificial death on the cross. Through this act, Jesus absorbed the consequences of sin, offering salvation and the opportunity for reconciliation with God to all who believe in Him. This theme is not only foundational to Christian doctrine but also deeply rooted in the themes of judgment and redemption seen throughout the Bible, including in the prophecies of Jeremiah.

In this chapter, we will explore how Jesus took upon Himself the judgment for sin, examining the biblical basis for this belief, the nature of His sacrifice, and the implications for salvation. Jesus' unique role as the one who bore God's judgment on behalf of humanity serves as the ultimate fulfillment of God's justice and mercy.

2. The Necessity of Judgment for Sin

To understand the significance of Jesus' role in bearing judgment, it is crucial to recognize the biblical principle that sin requires judgment. According to Scripture, sin is rebellion against God's law and nature, and it separates humanity from God. Throughout the Old Testament, including the prophecies of Jeremiah, we see that sin leads to consequences—judgment, exile, and separation from God's presence.

2.1 The Problem of Sin and Separation from God

The Bible teaches that all of humanity is guilty of sin, beginning with the fall of Adam and Eve in the Garden of

Eden. Their disobedience led to the entry of sin into the world, and from that moment, the relationship between God and humanity was broken. In Romans 3:23, Paul summarizes the human condition:

> "For all have sinned and fall short of the glory of God." (ESV)

Sin not only incurs guilt but also leads to spiritual death, which is the ultimate consequence of separation from God. In Romans 6:23, Paul emphasizes the seriousness of sin:

> "For the wages of sin is death, but the free gift of God is eternal life in Christ Jesus our Lord." (ESV)

Because God is perfectly holy and just, sin must be dealt with through judgment. Throughout the Old Testament, God's judgment against sin is illustrated through various means—exile, destruction, and death—but in the New Testament, the focus shifts to how Jesus absorbs this judgment on behalf of humanity.

2.2 God's Justice: The Need for Judgment

God's nature as just and holy means that sin cannot go unpunished. Just as Jeremiah prophesied about the coming judgment upon Judah for their sins, the New Testament emphasizes that all people are subject to divine judgment. In Hebrews 9:27, we read:

> "And just as it is appointed for man to die once, and after that comes judgment." (ESV)

Without addressing the problem of sin through justice, reconciliation between God and humanity would be impossible. This sets the stage for the role of Jesus as the one who bears the judgment on behalf of all who believe.

3. Jesus as the Substitute for Sin

The concept of Jesus taking upon Himself the judgment for sin is central to the Christian understanding of the atonement. Jesus, who was sinless, became the perfect substitute for humanity, taking on the punishment that was deserved by others.

3.1 The Lamb of God: Jesus as the Ultimate Sacrifice

In the Old Testament, the sacrificial system was instituted to atone for sin. Animals were sacrificed as substitutes for the people's sins, symbolically taking on the judgment that the people deserved. However, these sacrifices were temporary and could not fully remove sin. In Jesus, Christians believe, God provided the ultimate and final sacrifice—one that would deal with sin once and for all.

John the Baptist recognized this role when he saw Jesus and declared in John 1:29:

> "Behold, the Lamb of God, who takes away the sin of the world!" (ESV)

Jesus, as the "Lamb of God," fulfills the sacrificial system by offering His own life as a substitute for sinners. Unlike the animals sacrificed in the Old Covenant, which had to be offered repeatedly, Jesus' sacrifice is once for all, fully satisfying the demands of God's justice.

3.2 Jesus as the Sin-Bearer

Paul's letters emphasize that Jesus became the bearer of sin, absorbing the judgment that was due to humanity. In 2 Corinthians 5:21, Paul writes:

> "For our sake he made him to be sin who knew no sin, so that in him we might become the righteousness of God." (ESV)

This verse expresses the profound exchange that took place on the cross: Jesus, who was sinless, became sin on behalf of humanity, bearing the full weight of divine judgment. In return, those who believe in Him receive His righteousness, allowing them to be reconciled to God.

The imagery of substitution is also seen in Isaiah 53, a passage often referred to as the "Suffering Servant" prophecy. In Isaiah 53:4-5, the prophet foretells the suffering of the Messiah, who would take upon Himself the punishment for sin:

> "Surely he has borne our griefs and carried our sorrows... But he was pierced for our transgressions; he was crushed for our iniquities; upon him was the chastisement that brought us peace, and with his wounds we are healed." (ESV)

For Christians, this prophecy is fulfilled in the person of Jesus, whose sacrificial death provided healing and redemption for humanity by bearing the judgment that sin demands.

4. Jesus' Death on the Cross: The Ultimate Act of Judgment and Redemption

The crucifixion of Jesus is central to the Christian faith because it represents both the outpouring of God's judgment on sin and the means of redemption for those who believe. On the cross, Jesus bore the wrath of God, taking the full penalty for sin, and through His death, He opened the way for salvation.

4.1 The Wrath of God Satisfied

At the cross, the judgment for sin was poured out on Jesus, who willingly took on this role as a sacrifice. In Christian theology, Jesus' death is seen as a propitiation—a sacrifice that turns away God's wrath. In Romans 3:25, Paul describes Jesus as the one whom God put forward as a propitiation by His blood:

> "Whom God put forward as a propitiation by his blood, to be received by faith. This was to show God's righteousness, because in his divine forbearance he had passed over former sins." (ESV)

Jesus' sacrifice on the cross satisfied the demands of justice, allowing God to remain just while also justifying those who place their faith in Him. Through His death, the wrath of God was turned away, and the barrier of sin that separated humanity from God was removed.

4.2 Redemption through His Blood

The concept of redemption is closely tied to Jesus' role in bearing judgment. To redeem is to purchase or set free by paying a price, and in the case of Jesus, His blood—the life He gave on the cross—was the price paid for humanity's salvation.

In Ephesians 1:7, Paul emphasizes the redemptive power of Jesus' sacrifice:

> "In him we have redemption through his blood, the forgiveness of our trespasses, according to the riches of his grace." (ESV)

Jesus' death accomplished not only the removal of sin's penalty but also the restoration of the relationship between God and humanity. Through His death, believers are set free from the bondage of sin and death and are brought into a new life of grace.

5. The Resurrection: Victory Over Judgment and Death

While Jesus' death on the cross is central to the theme of judgment, His resurrection is equally vital in the Christian understanding of salvation. The resurrection is seen as God's vindication of Jesus and the final victory over sin, death, and judgment.

5.1 The Resurrection as God's Approval

The resurrection of Jesus from the dead is the ultimate affirmation that His sacrifice was accepted by God. It demonstrates that the judgment Jesus bore on the cross was sufficient and that sin and death had been defeated. In Romans 4:25, Paul connects the resurrection with justification:

> "He was delivered up for our trespasses and raised for our justification." (ESV)

The resurrection is proof that believers are justified—declared righteous—before God because the penalty for sin has been paid in full.

5.2 The Resurrection and Eternal Life

Through His resurrection, Jesus conquers death, offering the promise of eternal life to all who believe. Just as death was the consequence of sin, Jesus' resurrection breaks the power of death and opens the door to eternal life. In 1 Corinthians 15:54-57, Paul celebrates this victory:

> "Death is swallowed up in victory. O death, where is your victory? O death, where is your sting?... But thanks be to God, who gives us the victory through our Lord Jesus Christ." (ESV)

Jesus' resurrection marks the triumph of life over death and provides believers with the assurance that, because of His victory, they too will be raised to eternal life with God.

6. Salvation Through Faith: Accepting Jesus' Sacrifice

The salvation that Jesus offers through His bearing of judgment is made available to all who believe. Faith in Jesus is the means by which individuals receive the benefits of His sacrificial death and resurrection. Paul emphasizes the importance of faith in receiving salvation in Ephesians 2:8-9:

> "For by grace you have been saved through faith. And this is not your own doing; it is the gift of God, not a result of works, so that no one may boast." (ESV)

Salvation is a gift, freely given through God's grace, and it is received by placing one's trust in Jesus' work on the cross.

6.1 The Offer of Forgiveness

For those who accept Jesus' sacrifice, the judgment for sin is removed, and they receive complete forgiveness. In Colossians 2:13-14, Paul describes the wiping away of sin's record:

> "And you, who were dead in your trespasses... God made alive together with him, having forgiven us all our trespasses, by canceling the record of debt that stood against us with its legal demands. This he set aside, nailing it to the cross." (ESV)

The forgiveness offered through Jesus is total and final, bringing freedom from guilt and the assurance of a restored relationship with God.

6.2 New Life in Christ

In addition to forgiveness, those who place their faith in Jesus experience new life. They are spiritually reborn, transformed from being under judgment to being children of God. In 2 Corinthians 5:17, Paul declares:

> "Therefore, if anyone is in Christ, he is a new creation. The old has passed away; behold, the new has come." (ESV)

This new life includes not only freedom from the penalty of sin but also the indwelling presence of the Holy Spirit, empowering believers to live in accordance with God's will.

7. Conclusion: Jesus as the Ultimate Bearer of Judgment and Source of Salvation

In Jesus Christ, the judgment for sin is fully borne, and through His death and resurrection, the door to salvation is opened for all who believe. Jesus' willingness to take on the punishment for humanity's sin demonstrates both God's justice and His profound love and mercy. Through His sacrifice, the demands of divine justice are satisfied, and the way is made for forgiveness, redemption, and eternal life.

For Christians, Jesus stands as the ultimate fulfillment of the prophecies of judgment and redemption seen throughout the Old Testament, including the writings of Jeremiah. Just as God judged the sins of Judah but promised restoration, in Jesus, God offers judgment for sin and the ultimate restoration through salvation. Those who place their faith in Jesus are freed from the consequences of sin and are given the promise of eternal life with God.

The Promise of Restoration

1. Introduction: Restoration in the Prophecies of Jeremiah

The Book of Jeremiah is characterized by powerful themes of judgment and exile, but it also contains one of the most profound messages of hope in the Old Testament: the promise of restoration. While Jeremiah's prophecies warn of the destruction of Jerusalem and the exile of the people of Judah due to their persistent disobedience, they also look beyond the immediate judgment to a future where God's people will be restored to their land, renewed in their relationship with God, and transformed by a new covenant. For Christians, these promises of restoration point toward the ultimate redemption found in Jesus Christ, who fulfills God's plan to redeem not just Israel but all of humanity.

This chapter explores how the promises of restoration in Jeremiah foreshadow the redemption and reconciliation made possible through Christ. By examining the key elements of these promises—return from exile, spiritual renewal, and the New Covenant—we can see how Jeremiah's prophecies find their fulfillment in the life, death, and resurrection of Jesus.

2. The Promised Restoration of Judah: A Return from Exile

One of the central themes of restoration in Jeremiah is the promise that God will bring His people back from exile and restore them to their land. The Babylonian exile was a direct result of Judah's persistent idolatry, injustice, and rejection of God's covenant. Yet, even in the midst of warnings about the coming judgment, God assured the people that their exile would not be the end of their story. He promised to gather them back to their homeland, indicating not only a physical return but also a spiritual renewal of their relationship with God.

2.1 The Hope of Return

In Jeremiah 29:10-14, God declares His intention to restore His people after their period of exile in Babylon:

> "For thus says the Lord: When seventy years are completed for Babylon, I will visit you, and I will fulfill to you my promise and bring you back to this place. For I know the plans I have for you, declares the Lord, plans for welfare and not for evil, to give you a future and a hope. Then you will call upon me and come and pray to me, and I will hear you. You will seek me and find me, when you seek me with all your heart. I will be found by you, declares the Lord, and I will restore your fortunes and gather you from all the nations and all the places where I have driven you, declares the Lord, and I will bring you back to the place from which I sent you into exile." (ESV)

This passage offers hope and assurance that the exile is not permanent. God promises that, after a set time of seventy years, He will bring His people back to the land of Judah. The physical return from exile symbolizes God's faithfulness to His covenant and His desire to restore the people to their rightful place as His chosen nation.

2.2 The Gathering of the Scattered People

Jeremiah frequently uses the imagery of gathering the scattered flock to describe God's promise of restoration. In Jeremiah 23:3, God assures the people that He will act as a shepherd, gathering His scattered sheep:

> "Then I will gather the remnant of my flock out of all the countries where I have driven them, and I will bring them back to their fold, and they shall be fruitful and multiply." (ESV)

This promise of gathering reflects both a literal return to the land and a deeper spiritual restoration. God's people had been scattered because of their disobedience, but in His mercy, He promises to gather them once again, restoring the covenant relationship between Him and His people.

3. Spiritual Renewal: A Transformed Relationship with God

In Jeremiah's prophecies, God's promise of restoration goes beyond the physical return from exile to a profound spiritual renewal of His people. The exile was a result of the people's repeated disobedience, idolatry, and rejection of God's laws. Jeremiah speaks not only of God bringing them back to the land but also of transforming their hearts and minds, enabling them to live in faithful obedience. This spiritual renewal is rooted in God's desire for a deeper, more intimate relationship with His people—a transformation that finds its ultimate fulfillment in the New Covenant and in the person of Jesus Christ.

3.1 Circumcision of the Heart: Internal Transformation

Jeremiah addresses the need for an internal transformation, often described as the "circumcision of the heart." The people of Judah had outwardly participated in religious rituals, but their hearts were far from God. This disconnect between external religious observance and inner devotion was a major reason for their downfall.

In Jeremiah 4:4, the prophet calls the people to turn back to God through repentance and internal renewal:

> "Circumcise yourselves to the Lord; remove the foreskin of your hearts, O men of Judah and inhabitants of Jerusalem; lest my wrath go forth like fire, and burn with none to quench it, because of the evil of your deeds." (ESV)

The concept of "circumcision of the heart" emphasizes the need for a true change in the heart and mind, a deep spiritual transformation that goes beyond outward religious practices. God desired His people to be inwardly devoted to Him, with hearts that were softened and open to His commandments.

This internal transformation, where God's law is not merely external but written on the hearts of His people, finds its fullest expression in Jeremiah's prophecy of the New Covenant. The promise of spiritual renewal is central to the idea that God's people would be able to live in true obedience, not through external compulsion, but through a heart aligned with God's will.

3.2 The New Covenant: A Promise of Lasting Renewal

Perhaps the most significant promise of spiritual renewal in Jeremiah is found in Jeremiah 31:31-34, where God speaks of establishing a New Covenant with His people. This New Covenant would be different from the Mosaic Covenant, which the people had repeatedly broken. Rather than being based on external laws, the New Covenant would involve a deep, internal change, where God's law would be written on the hearts of the people, leading to true and lasting obedience.

In Jeremiah 31:33, God declares:

> "For this is the covenant that I will make with the house of Israel after those days, declares the Lord: I will put my law within them, and I will write it on their hearts. And I will be their God, and they shall be my people." (ESV)

This New Covenant marks a significant shift in the relationship between God and His people. It promises an intimate, personal relationship, where God's law is not merely a set of external rules but becomes a part of the very fabric of the people's lives. This internalization of God's law is central to the spiritual renewal that Jeremiah envisions. Under this New Covenant, the people will no longer struggle to follow God's commands through their own effort but will be empowered to do so by a transformed heart.

The New Covenant also includes the promise of complete forgiveness of sins, as seen in Jeremiah 31:34:

> "For I will forgive their iniquity, and I will remember their sin no more." (ESV)

This forgiveness would allow the people to have a fresh start, free from the guilt and shame of their past sins. It speaks to God's mercy and His desire to reconcile with His people, not just through external rituals, but through an intimate, heart-changing relationship.

4. Fulfillment of Restoration in Christ: The Ultimate Spiritual Renewal

For Christians, the promises of restoration and spiritual renewal in Jeremiah find their ultimate fulfillment in Jesus Christ. Jesus is seen as the mediator of the New Covenant, the one who brings about the internal transformation and forgiveness of sins that Jeremiah prophesied. Through His life, death, and resurrection, Jesus inaugurates the New Covenant, offering spiritual renewal to all who believe in Him.

4.1 Jesus as the Mediator of the New Covenant

The New Testament explicitly identifies Jesus as the one who fulfills Jeremiah's promise of the New Covenant. In Luke 22:20, during the Last Supper, Jesus declares:

> "This cup that is poured out for you is the new covenant in my blood." (ESV)

Jesus' death on the cross is seen as the means by which the New Covenant is established. Through His sacrificial death, Jesus provides the forgiveness of sins that Jeremiah had promised, and through His resurrection, He offers new life— a transformed relationship with God. This New Covenant is not just for Israel but for all people, extending the promise of spiritual renewal to the entire world.

4.2 The Law Written on the Hearts of Believers

The internalization of God's law, as prophesied by Jeremiah, is realized through the work of the Holy Spirit in the lives of believers. In Christian theology, the Holy Spirit plays a central role in writing God's law on the hearts of believers, enabling them to live in obedience and in relationship with God. Paul speaks of this transformation in Romans 8:2-4:

> "For the law of the Spirit of life has set you free in Christ Jesus from the law of sin and death... in order that the righteous requirement of the law might be fulfilled in us, who walk not according to the flesh but according to the Spirit." (ESV)

This passage reflects the spiritual renewal promised in Jeremiah, where the law is no longer an external code but is written on the hearts of believers through the work of the Holy Spirit. Through Jesus, believers are empowered to live in a way that reflects God's will, fulfilling the righteous requirements of the law in a new, Spirit-empowered way.

4.3 The Forgiveness of Sins and Reconciliation with God

The New Covenant also fulfills the promise of forgiveness and reconciliation with God. Through Jesus' atoning sacrifice, the sins of believers are fully forgiven, just as Jeremiah had prophesied. In Hebrews 10:16-17, the writer echoes Jeremiah's words, applying them to the work of Christ:

> "This is the covenant that I will make with them after those days, declares the Lord: I will put my laws on their hearts, and write them on their minds... I will remember their sins and their lawless deeds no more." (ESV)

This forgiveness brings about the ultimate restoration of the relationship between God and humanity. No longer separated by sin, believers are welcomed into a reconciled, intimate relationship with God, experiencing the full benefits of the New Covenant.

5. Conclusion: The Promise of Restoration Fulfilled in Christ

The promises of restoration in Jeremiah speak to God's enduring faithfulness and His desire to restore His people, both physically and spiritually. While the immediate context of these promises involved the return of the people of Judah from Babylonian exile, the deeper significance of these prophecies points to a future where God would establish a New Covenant with His people—one that would involve the transformation of their hearts and the forgiveness of their sins.

For Christians, the ultimate fulfillment of these promises is found in Jesus Christ, who establishes the New Covenant through His death and resurrection. In Christ, the law is written on the hearts of believers, and they experience the spiritual renewal and forgiveness that Jeremiah prophesied. Through Jesus, the restoration is not merely a return to a physical land but a return to a right relationship with God—an eternal restoration that offers peace, reconciliation, and new life.

179

CHAPTER 06

THE DIVINE KING

1. Introduction: The Sovereign Rule of God in Jeremiah

The Book of Jeremiah contains some of the most powerful declarations of God's sovereignty and kingship over all creation. One such declaration is found in Jeremiah 10:10:

> "But the Lord is the true God; he is the living God and the everlasting King. At his wrath the earth quakes, and the nations cannot endure his indignation." (ESV)

In this verse, God is presented not only as the true and living God but also as the everlasting King—a title that points to His eternal reign and supreme authority over the world. For Jeremiah, this declaration of God's kingship stands in contrast to the false gods and idols worshiped by the surrounding nations, which are lifeless and powerless.

For Christians, this image of God as the everlasting King finds its ultimate fulfillment in Jesus Christ, who is revealed in the New Testament as the King of kings and Lord of lords. In this chapter, we will explore the nature of God's kingship as described in Jeremiah, and how Christians see this as a foreshadowing of the divine kingship of Jesus. We will examine Jesus' role as the divine King, the fulfillment of messianic expectations, and the implications of His kingship for the Christian faith.

2. The Lord as the Everlasting King in Jeremiah

Throughout the Book of Jeremiah, God's sovereign rule is emphasized, especially in contrast to the lifeless idols that the people of Judah were tempted to worship. Jeremiah repeatedly reminds the people that their God is not like the false gods of the nations; He is the living and eternal King who rules over all creation.

2.1 The True and Living God

In Jeremiah 10:6-7, the prophet exalts the uniqueness of God's kingship over the nations:

> "There is none like you, O Lord; you are great, and your name is great in might. Who would not fear you, O King of the nations? For this is your due; for among all the wise ones of the nations and in all their kingdoms there is none like you." (ESV)

Here, God is described as the "King of the nations," a title that emphasizes His supreme authority not just over Israel, but over all the kingdoms of the earth. This kingship is rooted in God's power and wisdom, which far surpass the wisdom of the rulers of the nations.

In the same chapter, Jeremiah contrasts God's kingship with the futility of idols, pointing out that these man-made gods cannot speak, move, or act. In Jeremiah 10:11, the prophet declares:

> "Thus shall you say to them: 'The gods who did not make the heavens and the earth shall perish from the earth and from under the heavens.'" (ESV)

The impotence of idols highlights the absolute power and authority of the Lord as the living God, the Creator of the universe. His reign is not limited by time or space, and His kingdom is everlasting. Jeremiah underscores that God's kingship is eternal, unchallenged, and unchanging, making Him the rightful ruler over all.

2.2 God's Judgment and Authority

As the everlasting King, God's authority extends to His role as judge. In Jeremiah 10:10, the prophet notes that at God's wrath, the earth quakes, and the nations cannot endure His indignation. This portrayal of God's wrath reveals His role as the righteous judge who holds the nations accountable for their actions.

God's kingship is not only a matter of sovereignty but also of divine justice. Throughout Jeremiah, God's judgment is seen as an expression of His kingship, where He holds both Israel and the nations to account for their sins. His authority to judge flows from His role as the Creator and King, and His judgments are a demonstration of His righteous rule.

3. The Messianic Expectation: A Coming King

Jeremiah, along with other prophets in the Old Testament, points to a future ruler from the line of David who will reign with justice and righteousness. This messianic expectation is rooted in the promises made to David in the Davidic Covenant, where God assures David that his descendants will always sit on the throne of Israel.

3.1 The Righteous Branch from David's Line

In Jeremiah 23:5-6, the prophet gives a clear messianic prophecy about a coming King:

> "Behold, the days are coming, declares the Lord, when I will raise up for David a righteous Branch, and he shall

reign as king and deal wisely, and shall execute justice and righteousness in the land. In his days Judah will be saved, and Israel will dwell securely. And this is the name by which he will be called: 'The Lord is our righteousness.'" (ESV)

This prophecy speaks of a future King from the line of David who will reign with wisdom, justice, and righteousness. For Christians, this prophecy points directly to Jesus Christ, who is seen as the fulfillment of the messianic hope. Jesus is the promised King who would bring salvation not only to Israel but to the entire world.

The title given to this King—"The Lord is our righteousness"—emphasizes the divine nature of the messianic ruler. This title not only highlights the King's role in bringing justice but also points to the deeper truth that this King will embody the righteousness of God Himself.

3.2 The Hope of the Divine King

The hope for a future King was deeply rooted in the covenant promises made to Israel, particularly the promise of a Davidic ruler. This King was expected to bring about a time of peace, justice, and restoration for God's people. Jeremiah's prophecy of the "righteous Branch" reflects the longing for a ruler who would fulfill these promises and bring about the full realization of God's kingdom on earth.

For the people of Israel, this messianic hope was not only a political hope but also a spiritual one. The coming King would be a shepherd who would gather the scattered flock, restore the covenant relationship with God, and bring true peace. In the New Testament, Christians believe that this hope is ultimately realized in Jesus Christ, the Divine King who inaugurates the Kingdom of God.

4. Jesus as the Fulfillment of the Divine Kingship

In the New Testament, Jesus is presented as the fulfillment of the messianic promises, including those found in Jeremiah. He is revealed as the Divine King, whose reign transcends political boundaries and earthly kingdoms. His kingship is marked by justice, righteousness, and a deep connection to the divine.

4.1 Jesus as the King of Kings

Throughout the New Testament, Jesus is referred to as the King. In the Gospels, the theme of Jesus' kingship is evident from the very beginning, as seen in the story of the Magi coming to worship Him, asking, "Where is he who has been born king of the Jews?" (Matthew 2:2, ESV). Jesus' kingship is further emphasized throughout His ministry, where He speaks of the Kingdom of God and performs miracles that demonstrate His authority over creation.

The title King of kings and Lord of lords is given to Jesus in the Book of Revelation, underscoring His supreme authority over all other rulers and powers. In Revelation 19:16, Jesus is described as:

> "On his robe and on his thigh he has a name written, King of kings and Lord of lords." (ESV)

This title emphasizes Jesus' divine authority, declaring Him as the ultimate ruler over all the earth. His kingship is not limited to Israel but extends to the entire world, fulfilling the prophecy of the everlasting King in Jeremiah.

4.2 Jesus' Reign of Justice and Righteousness

As the promised Messiah and Divine King, Jesus' reign is characterized by justice and righteousness—attributes that Jeremiah had prophesied about the coming King. Jesus demonstrated this in His ministry by healing the sick, defending the marginalized, and proclaiming the good news of the Kingdom of God.

Jesus' reign is not only about justice but also about restoring the broken relationship between God and humanity. Through His sacrificial death on the cross, Jesus brings about reconciliation, offering salvation to all who believe in Him. In doing so, Jesus fulfills the messianic hope of bringing peace and salvation, not just to Israel, but to the whole world.

4.3 The Eternal Kingship of Christ

One of the most profound aspects of Jesus' kingship is its eternal nature. Like the everlasting King described in Jeremiah, Jesus' reign is without end. In Hebrews 1:8, we read of the eternal nature of Jesus' kingship:

> "But of the Son he says, 'Your throne, O God, is forever and ever, the scepter of uprightness is the scepter of your kingdom.'" (ESV)

Jesus' kingship transcends time and space, marking Him as the Divine King whose reign will never end. For Christians, the eternal kingship of Christ means that He is always reigning, even now, as the sovereign ruler of all creation. His kingdom is not of this world, but it is advancing in the hearts of those who follow Him, and it will be fully realized when He returns to establish His eternal reign.

5. The Implications of Christ's Kingship for Christian Life

The recognition of Jesus as the Divine King has profound implications for Christian life and faith. Jesus' kingship calls believers to submit to His rule, live according to His justice and righteousness, and participate in His kingdom's mission.

5.1 Submission to the Divine King

Acknowledging Jesus as the King of kings means submitting to His authority in every area of life. As Christians, this submission involves aligning one's life with Jesus' teachings, following His commands, and living as citizens of His kingdom. In Matthew 6:33, Jesus urges His followers:

> "But seek first the kingdom of God and his righteousness, and all these things will be added to you." (ESV)

Living under Jesus' kingship means prioritizing His kingdom and righteousness in one's daily life, trusting that His reign brings peace, justice, and provision.

5.2 Living in the Reality of God's Kingdom

For Christians, Jesus' kingship is not just a future hope but a present reality. Believers are called to live in the reality of God's kingdom here and now, participating in the mission of bringing justice, mercy, and love to the world. As citizens of Jesus' kingdom, Christians are ambassadors of His reign, tasked with sharing the good news of the King and working to make His kingdom visible in the world.

6. Conclusion: Jesus as the Divine King Fulfilled

The promise of an everlasting King in Jeremiah points to the nature of God as the sovereign ruler of all creation. For Christians, this kingship finds its ultimate fulfillment in Jesus Christ, who is revealed as the King of kings and Lord of lords. Jesus' divine kingship is not only a fulfillment of messianic expectations but also a source of hope and salvation for the entire world.

Through His life, death, and resurrection, Jesus brings about the reign of justice and righteousness that Jeremiah prophesied. His kingdom is eternal, and His rule offers peace, reconciliation, and salvation to all who submit to His authority. As the Divine King, Jesus calls His followers to live under His lordship, participating in His mission and advancing His kingdom in the world.

The Everlasting King in Jeremiah

1. Introduction: The Kingship of God in the Book of Jeremiah

Throughout the Book of Jeremiah, the prophet emphasizes the sovereignty and supremacy of God as the ultimate King, not only over Israel but over all nations. In contrast to the false gods worshiped by the nations and the failed human kings who ruled Israel and Judah, Jeremiah consistently presents God as the everlasting King—the true, living God who exercises authority, power, and justice over the entire world.

This portrayal of God's kingship in Jeremiah serves as a theological anchor for the prophet's message. Despite the political turmoil, impending exile, and the failure of human leaders, Jeremiah points to God as the rightful and enduring ruler of all. This chapter explores how Jeremiah presents God as the ultimate King, examines His rule over Israel and the nations, and discusses the implications of this kingship for understanding divine sovereignty in the context of judgment and redemption.

2. God as the True and Living King

Jeremiah's portrayal of God as King stands in stark contrast to the lifeless idols and corrupt kings that surrounded the people of Israel. In a time when many of the surrounding nations worshiped idols and when Judah's own leaders were failing to uphold justice and righteousness, Jeremiah reasserts God's position as the one true and living King.

2.1 God's Sovereignty Over Idols and Nations

A key element of Jeremiah's message is the distinction between the true, living God and the false gods or idols worshiped by the nations. In Jeremiah 10:10, Jeremiah boldly declares:

> "But the Lord is the true God; he is the living God and the everlasting King. At his wrath the earth quakes, and the nations cannot endure his indignation." (ESV)

This verse highlights several important aspects of God's kingship: He is the true God, in contrast to the false gods of the nations; He is the living God, possessing life and power, unlike lifeless idols; and He is the everlasting King, whose rule is eternal and unchanging.

In Jeremiah 10:5, the prophet mocks the idols made by human hands, describing them as powerless and immobile:

> "Their idols are like scarecrows in a cucumber field, and they cannot speak; they have to be carried, for they cannot walk. Do not be afraid of them, for they cannot do evil, neither is it in them to do good." (ESV)

Jeremiah contrasts these lifeless idols with the living God, whose power is unmatched. God is not limited to a particular territory or people; His kingship extends over all nations and creation itself. The earth trembles at His voice, and the nations are subject to His judgment and rule.

2.2 God's Eternal Kingship

The term everlasting King signifies that God's rule is not bound by time or circumstance. Unlike human kings, whose reigns are temporary and flawed, God's kingship is eternal. His authority does not diminish, and He will remain sovereign forever.

In Jeremiah 10:6-7, the prophet declares the uniqueness and majesty of God's kingship:

> "There is none like you, O Lord; you are great, and your name is great in might. Who would not fear you, O King of the nations? For this is your due; for among all the wise

ones of the nations and in all their kingdoms there is none like you." (ESV)

Here, God is not just the King of Israel; He is the King of the nations. His rule transcends national boundaries, and His wisdom and might surpass all human rulers. The fear and reverence due to God as King are universal, as no other king or god can compare to Him.

3. God's Kingship Over Israel: The Covenant King

While God's kingship extends over all nations, Jeremiah also presents God as the Covenant King of Israel. This kingship is rooted in the covenant relationship between God and His people, established at Mount Sinai and renewed throughout Israel's history.

3.1 God as Israel's Covenant King

From the time of the Exodus, God was regarded as Israel's King. He led them out of slavery in Egypt, gave them the law at Mount Sinai, and promised to be their God if they would be His people. This covenantal relationship is foundational to the understanding of God's kingship over Israel.

In Jeremiah 11:3-4, God reminds the people of the terms of the covenant:

> "Cursed be the man who does not hear the words of this covenant that I commanded your fathers when I

brought them out of the land of Egypt, from the iron furnace, saying, 'Listen to my voice, and do all that I command you. So shall you be my people, and I will be your God.'" (ESV)

Despite Israel's repeated rebellion and failure to uphold the covenant, God remained faithful as their King. Jeremiah's message often highlights the tension between God's covenant faithfulness and Israel's unfaithfulness, emphasizing that their ultimate hope lies not in human rulers but in their divine King.

3.2 The Rejection of God's Kingship by Israel's Leaders

One of the major themes in Jeremiah is the failure of Israel's human leaders, particularly the kings of Judah, to submit to God's rule. The kings of Judah were supposed to be representatives of God's kingship, ruling in justice and righteousness according to His law. However, many of these kings led the people into idolatry and disobedience, effectively rejecting God's rule.

In Jeremiah 22:1-5, the prophet confronts the king of Judah, urging him to rule with justice and obedience to God's covenant:

> "Thus says the Lord: 'Do justice and righteousness, and deliver from the hand of the oppressor him who has been robbed. And do no wrong or violence to the resident alien,

the fatherless, and the widow, nor shed innocent blood in this place... But if you will not obey these words, I swear by myself, declares the Lord, that this house shall become a desolation.'" (ESV)

The failure of Israel's kings to uphold justice and righteousness is a major reason for the judgment that Jeremiah predicts. Their rejection of God's kingship and their failure to lead the people in covenant faithfulness result in the destruction of Jerusalem and the exile of the people.

4. God's Kingship Over the Nations: Sovereign Judge

While God's kingship over Israel is central to Jeremiah's message, the prophet also emphasizes God's rule over the nations. God is not just the King of Israel; He is the sovereign ruler and judge of all the earth. Jeremiah frequently speaks of God's judgment on the nations, demonstrating that His authority extends far beyond the borders of Israel and Judah.

4.1 God's Judgment on the Nations

Throughout the latter chapters of Jeremiah, the prophet delivers oracles against various nations, including Egypt, Moab, Ammon, Edom, Babylon, and others. These prophecies reveal that the nations are accountable to God for their actions, and He will judge them for their wickedness and idolatry.

In Jeremiah 46:10, God's judgment on Egypt is described:

> "That day is the day of the Lord God of hosts, a day of vengeance, to avenge himself on his foes. The sword shall devour and be sated and drink its fill of their blood. For the Lord God of hosts holds a sacrifice in the north country by the river Euphrates." (ESV)

These oracles make it clear that God is not a tribal deity concerned only with Israel's affairs. He is the King of all nations, and His justice will be executed on a global scale.

4.2 God's Control Over History

Another key theme in Jeremiah's portrayal of God's kingship is His control over history and international events. The rise and fall of empires, including the Babylonian empire, are seen as being under God's sovereign control. In Jeremiah 27:6, God refers to the Babylonian king, Nebuchadnezzar, as "my servant," indicating that even the most powerful rulers are subject to His will:

> "Now I have given all these lands into the hand of Nebuchadnezzar, the king of Babylon, my servant, and I have given him also the beasts of the field to serve him." (ESV)

Nebuchadnezzar's conquests, including his invasion of Judah and the exile of its people, are portrayed not merely as political events but as part of God's divine plan. God, as the King of kings, directs the course of history according to His purposes.

5. The Promise of the Future King

Despite the judgment that Jeremiah pronounces on Israel and the nations, the prophet also points to a future hope. God's kingship is eternal, and He promises to restore His people and reign through a righteous King from the line of David. This messianic hope is central to the theme of restoration in Jeremiah.

5.1 The Righteous Branch

In Jeremiah 23:5-6, the prophet foretells the coming of a righteous Branch from the line of David:

> "Behold, the days are coming, declares the Lord, when I will raise up for David a righteous Branch, and he shall reign as king and deal wisely, and shall execute justice and righteousness in the land. In his days Judah will be saved, and Israel will dwell securely. And this is the name by which he will be called: 'The Lord is our righteousness.'" (ESV)

This prophecy points to a future King who will rule with justice and righteousness, in contrast to the corrupt kings of Jeremiah's time. For Christians, this prophecy is seen as fulfilled in Jesus Christ, the Divine King who brings salvation and righteousness to all.

6. Conclusion: God as the Everlasting King

Jeremiah's portrayal of God as the everlasting King reveals His sovereignty over all creation. God's kingship is not limited to Israel but extends to all nations, and His rule is characterized by justice, righteousness, and eternal faithfulness. Despite the failures of Israel's kings and the judgment that befell the nation, Jeremiah points to God's ultimate control over history and His promise of restoration through a future King.

For Christians, this future King is understood to be Jesus Christ, who embodies the divine kingship foretold by Jeremiah. As the King of kings and Lord of lords, Jesus fulfills the promise of a righteous and eternal King, whose reign brings salvation, justice, and peace to all who trust in Him.

Jesus as King

1. Introduction: The Kingship of Jesus in the New Testament

In the New Testament, Jesus is repeatedly described as a king, fulfilling the messianic prophecies of the Old Testament that foretold the coming of a righteous ruler who would reign over Israel and the nations. The kingship of Jesus is central to Christian theology, as it establishes Him as the fulfillment of the divine promises of a coming Messiah, a King who would restore God's people and establish an everlasting kingdom of righteousness and peace.

This chapter explores how the New Testament presents Jesus as King, examining key passages that highlight His authority, His relationship to Old Testament prophecies, and how His kingship is both spiritual and universal. Jesus' kingship is not limited to political or temporal power but encompasses the entire creation, fulfilling God's plan for redemption and establishing His eternal reign.

2. Jesus as the Fulfillment of Messianic Prophecies

Throughout the Old Testament, particularly in the writings of the prophets like Jeremiah and Isaiah, the hope of a coming King from the line of David is a recurring theme. This King, often referred to as the Messiah or the Anointed One, would bring justice, peace, and salvation to Israel and the nations. Christians believe that Jesus is the fulfillment of these prophecies, embodying the divine kingship anticipated by the Jewish people.

2.1 Jesus as the Son of David

The lineage of Jesus is significant in affirming His messianic kingship, as He is identified as a descendant of David, the greatest king of Israel. In the Gospels, the title "Son of David" is often used to refer to Jesus, connecting Him directly to the Davidic Covenant in which God promised David that his descendants would rule forever.

In Matthew 1:1, the genealogy of Jesus begins with this assertion:

> "The book of the genealogy of Jesus Christ, the son of David, the son of Abraham." (ESV)

This establishes Jesus as the rightful heir to the throne of David, fulfilling the messianic expectation that the promised King would come from David's line, as prophesied in Jeremiah 23:5:

> "Behold, the days are coming, declares the Lord, when I will raise up for David a righteous Branch, and he shall reign as king and deal wisely, and shall execute justice and righteousness in the land." (ESV)

By emphasizing Jesus' Davidic lineage, the New Testament writers connect Him directly to the Old Testament prophecies that looked forward to a future King who would reign with justice and righteousness.

2.2 The Birth of a King

The account of Jesus' birth in the Gospels reinforces His identity as the King of Israel and the fulfillment of messianic prophecy. In Matthew 2:1-2, the wise men, or Magi, come from the east seeking the "King of the Jews":

> "Now after Jesus was born in Bethlehem of Judea in the days of Herod the king, behold, wise men from the east came to Jerusalem, saying, 'Where is he who has been born

king of the Jews? For we saw his star when it rose and have come to worship him.'" (ESV)

The Magi's recognition of Jesus as a king, even at His birth, reflects the understanding that His arrival marks the fulfillment of the long-awaited messianic King. The location of Jesus' birth in Bethlehem also fulfills the prophecy of Micah 5:2, which foretold that the ruler of Israel would come from Bethlehem, David's hometown.

3. Jesus as the Spiritual and Universal King

While Jesus is described as the rightful heir to David's throne, His kingship is not confined to political power or national boundaries. In the New Testament, Jesus' kingship is primarily spiritual, transcending earthly kingdoms and extending over the entire creation. He is not just the King of Israel but the King of kings and Lord of lords, whose reign brings spiritual liberation and eternal life.

3.1 Jesus Declares His Kingdom

Throughout His ministry, Jesus spoke about the Kingdom of God, a central theme of His teachings. However, Jesus made it clear that His kingdom was not of this world, distinguishing His reign from the political kingdoms of the earth. In John 18:36, Jesus tells Pilate:

> "My kingdom is not of this world. If my kingdom were of this world, my servants would have been fighting, that

I might not be delivered over to the Jews. But my kingdom is not from the world." (ESV)

This statement highlights the spiritual nature of Jesus' kingship. His reign is not maintained by force or earthly power but through the transformation of hearts and lives. Jesus' kingdom is built on righteousness, peace, and the truth of God's word, and His rule extends beyond the temporal realms to the eternal.

3.2 The Universal Kingship of Jesus

While Jesus is the fulfillment of the Jewish hope for a messianic King, the New Testament presents His kingship as universal, extending over all nations and peoples. In Philippians 2:9-11, Paul describes the exaltation of Jesus as the one to whom all creation will bow:

> "Therefore God has highly exalted him and bestowed on him the name that is above every name, so that at the name of Jesus every knee should bow, in heaven and on earth and under the earth, and every tongue confess that Jesus Christ is Lord, to the glory of God the Father." (ESV)

This passage affirms that Jesus' authority is not limited to a particular region or people group but is recognized by all creation. As the King of kings, Jesus is exalted to the highest place of honor, ruling over heaven and earth.

4. The Sacrificial Kingship of Jesus

One of the most profound aspects of Jesus' kingship, as presented in the New Testament, is His willingness to serve and sacrifice for His people. Unlike earthly kings who often seek power and wealth, Jesus demonstrates His kingship through humility, service, and ultimately, His sacrificial death on the cross. This sacrificial aspect of His reign sets Him apart from all other rulers and fulfills the Old Testament prophecies of the suffering Messiah.

4.1 The Humble King

Jesus' kingship is characterized by humility and service, qualities that were radically different from the expectations of a typical earthly king. In Matthew 21:5, Jesus enters Jerusalem riding on a donkey, fulfilling the prophecy of Zechariah 9:9:

> "Say to the daughter of Zion, 'Behold, your king is coming to you, humble, and mounted on a donkey, on a colt, the foal of a beast of burden.'" (ESV)

This scene, known as the Triumphal Entry, illustrates Jesus' humility as a king who comes to serve rather than to be served. His choice to enter the city on a donkey, rather than a war horse, symbolizes His peaceful reign and His mission to bring salvation through humility and sacrifice.

4.2 The King Who Dies for His People

At the heart of Jesus' kingship is His sacrificial death. Jesus willingly lays down His life for His people, a concept that stands in stark contrast to earthly kings who often demand the lives of their subjects. In John 10:11, Jesus describes Himself as the Good Shepherd who lays down His life for His sheep, revealing the depth of His love and commitment to His people.

Jesus' death on the cross is the ultimate expression of His kingship, as it is through His sacrifice that He conquers sin and death, bringing salvation to all who believe. In Revelation 5:9-10, Jesus is worshiped as the Lamb who was slain, and through His death, He establishes His kingdom:

> "Worthy are you to take the scroll and to open its seals, for you were slain, and by your blood you ransomed people for God from every tribe and language and people and nation, and you have made them a kingdom and priests to our God, and they shall reign on the earth." (ESV)

This passage highlights the redemptive nature of Jesus' kingship. Through His sacrificial death, He ransoms people from every nation, forming a kingdom of priests who will reign with Him.

5. The Return of the King: Jesus' Second Coming

The New Testament also speaks of Jesus' kingship in terms of His future return, when He will fully establish His reign over all creation. This is often referred to as the Second Coming or Parousia, where Jesus will return in glory to judge the nations and bring about the final consummation of His kingdom.

5.1 The King Who Will Judge

In Matthew 25:31-34, Jesus describes His return as the King who will judge the nations:

> "When the Son of Man comes in his glory, and all the angels with him, then he will sit on his glorious throne. Before him will be gathered all the nations, and he will separate people one from another as a shepherd separates the sheep from the goats." (ESV)

In this passage, Jesus is depicted as the reigning King who exercises judgment over all humanity. His authority as judge flows from His kingship, and He will determine the eternal destinies of all people based on their response to Him and their lives of faithfulness.

5.2 The Reign of Christ in the New Creation

In the final chapters of the New Testament, Jesus' kingship is fully realized in the new heavens and the new earth, where He reigns forever with His people. In Revelation 21:1-4, the Apostle John describes the new creation where God and His King, Jesus, dwell with humanity:

> "Then I saw a new heaven and a new earth, for the first heaven and the first earth had passed away... And I heard a loud voice from the throne saying, 'Behold, the dwelling place of God is with man. He will dwell with them, and they will be his people, and God himself will be with them as their God.'" (ESV)

Jesus' kingship culminates in the establishment of this new creation, where His rule is eternal, and His people enjoy perfect peace, justice, and communion with God. His reign brings the ultimate fulfillment of God's plan for humanity, as promised in the Old Testament.

6. Conclusion: Jesus as the Divine King Fulfilled

The New Testament presents Jesus as the King who fulfills the messianic prophecies of the Old Testament, particularly those concerning a righteous ruler from the line of David. Jesus embodies the qualities of the promised King—He is the Son of David, the King of kings, and the Lord of lords. His kingship is marked by humility, sacrifice, and universal authority, and it extends over all creation, both now and in the future.

Jesus' kingship is not merely political or temporal; it is deeply spiritual and eternal. He is the King who brings salvation, justice, and peace to all who follow Him, and His reign will be fully realized when He returns to establish His kingdom forever. For Christians, Jesus as King is the fulfillment of God's promises and the hope of redemption for all humanity.

The Reign of Christ

1. Introduction: The Beginning and Fulfillment of Christ's Reign

Christians believe that Jesus' reign as the eternal King began with His resurrection and ascension into heaven, marking the inauguration of His spiritual kingship over all creation. However, this reign is not yet fully realized in the present age, and Christians look forward to the day when Jesus will return in glory to establish His complete and final rule. This chapter explores the dual aspect of Christ's reign—how it was initiated at His resurrection and will be consummated at His second coming.

The tension between the "already" of Christ's present reign and the "not yet" of His future rule is a key theme in Christian theology. While Jesus is already King, His kingdom will be fully realized only when He returns to judge the living and the dead and to restore creation to its intended perfection.

2. The Inauguration of Christ's Reign: The Resurrection and Ascension

The resurrection of Jesus is the cornerstone of Christian faith and marks the beginning of His reign as the divine King. In His victory over death, Jesus not only proves His divine authority but also establishes His kingship over all things. The New Testament presents the resurrection as the pivotal moment when Jesus was exalted to His rightful place as Lord and King.

2.1 The Resurrection: Jesus' Victory Over Sin and Death

The resurrection of Jesus is seen as the ultimate demonstration of His divine authority and kingship. In Romans 1:4, Paul describes how Jesus was declared to be the Son of God in power through His resurrection:

> "... and was declared to be the Son of God in power according to the Spirit of holiness by his resurrection from the dead, Jesus Christ our Lord." (ESV)

The resurrection is not merely an event of personal triumph for Jesus; it is the moment when He decisively defeats the powers of sin, death, and evil. By rising from the dead, Jesus inaugurates His reign over a new creation, where death no longer holds dominion. This victory establishes Him as the King who rules over all, and through His resurrection, He begins to gather people into His kingdom.

2.2 The Ascension: Jesus' Enthronement as King

After His resurrection, Jesus ascended into heaven, where He took His place at the right hand of God, a position that signifies authority and kingship. The ascension is a crucial aspect of Christ's reign, as it marks His enthronement as the divine King who reigns over the heavens and the earth.

In Acts 1:9-11, we read the account of Jesus' ascension:

> "And when he had said these things, as they were looking on, he was lifted up, and a cloud took him out of their sight. And while they were gazing into heaven as he went, behold, two men stood by them in white robes, and said, 'Men of Galilee, why do you stand looking into heaven? This Jesus, who was taken up from you into heaven, will come in the same way as you saw him go into heaven.'" (ESV)

The ascension is not just Jesus' departure from earth but also His formal enthronement in the heavenly realms. In Ephesians 1:20-22, Paul describes how God raised Jesus from the dead and seated Him at His right hand, "far above all rule and authority and power and dominion," signifying that all things are under His feet. This passage emphasizes the authority and kingship of Jesus, who now reigns over all creation.

3. The Present Reign of Christ: The "Already"

While the full realization of Christ's kingdom is yet to come, Christians believe that Jesus is already reigning as King in the present age. This reign is spiritual in nature, as Jesus exercises His authority through the Church and the hearts of believers. The kingdom of God, which Jesus proclaimed during His earthly ministry, is both a present reality and a future hope.

3.1 The Kingdom of God in the Present

During His earthly ministry, Jesus frequently spoke of the kingdom of God, teaching that it was both "at hand" (Mark 1:15) and already present in the midst of His followers. The kingdom is not defined by geographical boundaries but by the rule of God in the hearts of those who follow Jesus. Through His teachings, miracles, and authority over demons, Jesus demonstrated the present power of His kingdom.

In Luke 17:20-21, Jesus explains the nature of the kingdom:

> "Being asked by the Pharisees when the kingdom of God would come, he answered them, 'The kingdom of God is not coming in ways that can be observed, nor will they say, 'Look, here it is!' or 'There!' for behold, the kingdom of God is in the midst of you.'" (ESV)

Jesus' words indicate that His reign has already begun, even if it is not yet fully visible. His kingdom is present wherever His will is done and wherever people submit to His lordship. This reign is extended through the Church, the body of Christ, which is tasked with proclaiming the good news of the kingdom and living out its values of love, justice, and peace.

3.2 Christ's Reign Through the Church

The Church plays a crucial role in the present reign of Christ. Christians believe that Jesus reigns as King through His people, who are called to be His representatives in the world. In Colossians 1:13, Paul describes how believers have been transferred into the kingdom of Christ:

> "He has delivered us from the domain of darkness and transferred us to the kingdom of his beloved Son." (ESV)

This transfer into Christ's kingdom means that believers are already living under His rule. As members of His kingdom, Christians are called to live in accordance with His teachings and to spread the message of His reign through acts of love, service, and justice.

Moreover, Jesus' reign is extended through the power of the Holy Spirit, who empowers believers to live out the values of His kingdom. The Spirit works in the lives of Christians to transform them into the image of Christ and to equip them for ministry in His name. Through the Church's witness, the kingdom of God continues to grow and advance in the present age.

4. The Future Reign of Christ: The "Not Yet"

While Jesus is currently reigning in a spiritual sense, Christians believe that His kingdom will be fully realized in the future, at the time of His second coming. This future reign will involve the complete fulfillment of God's promises, the final judgment of the world, and the establishment of a new heaven and a new earth where Jesus will reign forever.

4.1 The Return of Christ

The second coming of Jesus is central to Christian eschatology and is viewed as the moment when His reign will be visibly established over all creation. In Revelation 19:11-16, Jesus is depicted as a conquering King who returns to judge the nations and establish His rule:

> "Then I saw heaven opened, and behold, a white horse! The one sitting on it is called Faithful and True, and in righteousness he judges and makes war... On his robe and on his thigh he has a name written, King of kings and Lord of lords." (ESV)

This vivid imagery portrays Jesus as the triumphant King, returning to bring justice and righteousness to the earth. His return will mark the defeat of all evil and the full realization of His kingdom. The title King of kings and Lord of lords emphasizes that Jesus' authority will be recognized universally, as every knee will bow and every tongue will confess that He is Lord (Philippians 2:10-11).

4.2 The Final Judgment and New Creation

At the second coming, Jesus will not only return as King but also as Judge. In Matthew 25:31-34, Jesus describes His return as a time of judgment when He will separate the righteous from the wicked:

> "When the Son of Man comes in his glory, and all the angels with him, then he will sit on his glorious throne. Before him will be gathered all the nations, and he will separate people one from another as a shepherd separates the sheep from the goats." (ESV)

This judgment will determine the eternal destiny of all people. For those who have followed Christ, this is the moment of vindication, when they will enter into the fullness of His kingdom. For those who have rejected Him, it is a time of separation from His presence.

The final consummation of Christ's reign involves the creation of a new heaven and a new earth, where Jesus will reign forever. In Revelation 21:1-4, John describes the ultimate fulfillment of God's kingdom:

> "Then I saw a new heaven and a new earth, for the first heaven and the first earth had passed away... And I heard a loud voice from the throne saying, 'Behold, the dwelling place of God is with man. He will dwell with them, and they will be his people, and God himself will be with them as their

God. He will wipe away every tear from their eyes, and death shall be no more, neither shall there be mourning, nor crying, nor pain anymore, for the former things have passed away.'" (ESV)

In this vision, Jesus' reign is fully realized as He brings about the restoration of all things. The new creation is a place where God's perfect justice, peace, and love reign forever, and where death, sin, and suffering are no more. This is the ultimate goal of Christ's reign, where His victory over sin and death is made complete and His people dwell with Him in eternal joy.

5. The "Already" and the "Not Yet": Living in the Tension

The Christian understanding of Christ's reign involves living in the tension between the "already" and the "not yet". Jesus is already reigning as King, but the fullness of His kingdom is not yet visible. Christians are called to live in the present reality of Christ's reign, while also looking forward with hope to His return and the complete fulfillment of His kingdom.

5.1 Living Under Christ's Reign Now

In the present, Christians are called to acknowledge Jesus as their King and to live in obedience to His teachings. This involves submitting to His lordship in every area of life and participating in the mission of extending His kingdom through evangelism, discipleship, and acts of love and justice.

In Colossians 3:1-2, Paul encourages believers to live with their hearts set on Christ's kingdom:

> "If then you have been raised with Christ, seek the things that are above, where Christ is, seated at the right hand of God. Set your minds on things that are above, not on things that are on earth." (ESV)

This call to live in the reality of Christ's reign shapes the Christian life, orienting believers toward the values of the kingdom and giving them hope in the midst of a broken world.

5.2 Anticipating the Fullness of Christ's Reign

At the same time, Christians eagerly await the day when Christ will return to fully establish His reign. This anticipation gives believers hope, knowing that the brokenness and suffering of this world are temporary, and that Jesus will bring about the complete restoration of all things. The promise of Christ's return motivates Christians to live faithfully, knowing that their King will one day reign in glory.

6. Conclusion: The Reign of Christ Fulfilled

The reign of Jesus Christ began with His resurrection and ascension, marking the inauguration of His spiritual kingship over all creation. However, Christians believe that His reign will not be fully realized until His second coming, when He will return in glory to judge the nations and establish a new heaven and a new earth.

In the present, Jesus reigns in the hearts of His followers and through the work of the Church, advancing His kingdom on earth. But Christians also look forward to the day when His kingdom will be fully revealed, and His victory over sin, death, and evil will be complete. The reign of Christ is both a present reality and a future hope, calling believers to live in faithful obedience now and to anticipate the fulfillment of His eternal kingdom.

CHAPTER 07

JESUS AS THE ULTIMATE FUFLFILLMENT OF JUDGEMENT AND REDEMPTION

Jeremiah's message of suffering, judgment, and eventual redemption points toward the nature of divine justice and mercy. Jesus' life embodies these themes, taking them from the historical experience of Israel and applying them universally. The connection between the judgment that the people of Judah faced in Jeremiah's time and the judgment that Jesus bore on the cross is key to understanding the Christian view of redemption.

7.1 Jesus as the Embodiment of God's Justice

Throughout Jeremiah's prophecies, the message is clear: God is a God of justice. He will not overlook sin, nor will He allow rebellion to go unpunished. For Israel, the consequence of their idolatry and disobedience was exile. In the New Testament, the concept of judgment expands beyond the historical to the universal—sin brings judgment to all of humanity, not just Israel. Paul writes in Romans 3:23, "For all have sinned and fall short of the glory of God" (ESV), indicating that all people are subject to divine judgment because of sin.

However, in the Christian view, God's justice is satisfied through the atoning work of Jesus. On the cross, Jesus bore the judgment for humanity's sin, taking the punishment that was rightfully ours. In Romans 5:8-9, Paul elaborates:

> "But God shows his love for us in that while we were still sinners, Christ died for us. Since, therefore, we have now been justified by his blood, much more shall we be saved by him from the wrath of God." (ESV)

Jesus embodies God's justice by taking on the consequences of sin. This profound act of substitution satisfies the need for judgment while also revealing God's mercy.

7.2 Jesus as the Fulfillment of God's Promise of Redemption

The redemptive promises in Jeremiah, particularly the establishment of the New Covenant, are central to Christian belief. For Christians, Jesus fulfills the New Covenant that Jeremiah prophesied by bringing about a new relationship between God and humanity. Through His sacrifice, Jesus provides a way for humanity to be restored and reconciled to God.

In Luke 22:20, during the Last Supper, Jesus explicitly links His impending death with the New Covenant:

> "And likewise the cup after they had eaten, saying, 'This cup that is poured out for you is the new covenant in my blood.'" (ESV)

By instituting the New Covenant through His blood, Jesus fulfills the promise that God made through Jeremiah. The internal transformation that Jeremiah foretold—the law written on the hearts of God's people—comes to pass through the work of the Holy Spirit, which Christians believe is given to those who follow Christ. This internal transformation is not merely a matter of outward obedience but a deep spiritual renewal.

7.3 Jesus and the Reversal of Exile

In Jeremiah's time, exile was the ultimate sign of judgment, a physical and spiritual separation from God's presence. The return from exile symbolized God's faithfulness and the restoration of the covenant relationship. In a spiritual sense, Christians believe that Jesus' work on the cross and His resurrection reversed the ultimate exile—humanity's separation from God because of sin. Through His death and resurrection, Jesus paves the way for humanity to return to a right relationship with God.

In Colossians 1:13-14, Paul writes about the deliverance from spiritual exile:

> "He has delivered us from the domain of darkness and transferred us to the kingdom of his beloved Son, in whom we have redemption, the forgiveness of sins." (ESV)

This deliverance is seen as a kind of spiritual return from exile, a theme that echoes the promises in Jeremiah of God's people being brought back from the lands where they were scattered.

8. The Christian Life: Living in the Tension of Suffering and Redemption

The themes of suffering, judgment, and redemption that echo throughout Jeremiah's prophecies and find their fulfillment in Jesus also shape the way Christians understand their own lives. The Christian life is often seen as one lived in the tension between the reality of suffering and the hope of redemption.

8.1 Sharing in Christ's Sufferings

Christians believe that following Jesus often involves sharing in His sufferings. Just as Jesus endured suffering and judgment to bring about redemption, Christians are called to take up their crosses and follow Him, enduring hardship and trials for the sake of the Gospel. Paul writes in Philippians 3:10-11:

> "That I may know him and the power of his resurrection, and may share his sufferings, becoming like him in his death, that by any means possible I may attain the resurrection from the dead." (ESV)

This participation in suffering is not seen as pointless but as a path to greater spiritual growth and intimacy with Christ. Through suffering, Christians are conformed to the image of Christ, experiencing the deep spiritual renewal that comes from identifying with Him.

8.2 Living in the Reality of Redemption

While suffering is a part of the Christian life, the ultimate reality for believers is redemption. Just as Jeremiah's prophecies offered hope for restoration after the judgment, Christians believe that their suffering is temporary and will one day give way to eternal life with God. In 2 Corinthians 4:17, Paul reminds believers of this hope:

> "For this light momentary affliction is preparing for us an eternal weight of glory beyond all comparison." (ESV)

The redemption that Jesus brings is not only a future hope but also a present reality. Christians believe that through faith in Christ, they are already experiencing the firstfruits of this redemption—freedom from the power of sin, peace with God, and the indwelling presence of the Holy Spirit.

8.3 The Hope of Full Restoration

The final theme that connects Jeremiah's prophecies to the Christian experience is the hope of full restoration. Just as God promised to restore the fortunes of Israel after the exile, Christians look forward to the day when Christ will return and bring about the full and final restoration of creation. In Revelation 21:3-4, the apostle John describes this future restoration:

> "Behold, the dwelling place of God is with man. He will dwell with them, and they will be his people, and God himself will be with them as their God. He will wipe away every tear from their eyes, and death shall be no more, neither shall there be mourning, nor crying, nor pain anymore, for the former things have passed away." (ESV)

This future hope is the ultimate fulfillment of the promises of redemption in Jeremiah, where not only Israel but all of creation will be restored under the righteous reign of the Messiah.

9. Conclusion: Suffering, Judgment, and Redemption in the Light of Jesus

Jeremiah's prophecies of suffering, judgment, and redemption speak to the fundamental truths of the human condition—sin brings judgment, yet God's desire is always for restoration. In the life, death, and resurrection of Jesus, these themes find their fullest expression. Jesus' willingness to endure suffering and judgment for the sake of humanity provides the ultimate path to redemption, both for individuals and for the entire world.

For Christians, the story of Jeremiah is not simply a historical account of Israel's rebellion and exile but a powerful foreshadowing of the redemption that comes through Christ. Like the people of Israel, humanity has strayed from God and faces the consequences of sin. Yet, just as God promised to restore His people after their exile, He promises eternal restoration through Jesus.

Living in this reality of redemption shapes the Christian life, offering hope in the midst of suffering and pointing to the ultimate fulfillment of God's plan—a new creation where judgment is no more, and God's people live in perfect communion with Him. Through Jesus, the cycle of judgment and exile is broken, and the promise of redemption and restoration is made available to all who believe.

CHAPTER 08

JEREMIAH AND THE DIVINITY OF CHRIST

The Book of Jeremiah is filled with rich prophetic imagery, divine judgment, promises of hope, and the vision of restoration that resonates deeply within Christian theology. For Christians, the themes found in Jeremiah are more than just historical oracles directed toward the people of Judah; they are seen as prophecies pointing toward the ultimate fulfillment in the person of Jesus Christ. Central to this belief is the understanding that Jesus embodies the fulfillment of Jeremiah's prophecies, not only as a descendant of David, but as the divine Son of God who brings salvation, justice, and restoration to all.

1. The Branch of Righteousness: Jesus as the Messianic King

One of the clearest messianic prophecies in Jeremiah is the promise of the Branch of Righteousness in Jeremiah 23:5-6, which foretells the coming of a King from the line of David who will reign with wisdom, justice, and righteousness. For Christians, this promise is fulfilled in Jesus, who is seen as the true King and Messiah, reigning over an eternal kingdom. Jesus' life, ministry, and sacrificial death are seen as the means by which He brings salvation not only to Israel but to all humanity.

The title "The Lord is our righteousness" reflects Jesus' divine nature, indicating that He is more than just a human king—He embodies the righteousness of God. This connection underscores the Christian belief that Jesus is not only a messianic figure but also the divine Son of God who brings about the ultimate justice and salvation foretold by Jeremiah.

2. The New Covenant: Jesus as the Mediator of a Transformative Relationship

Another key element in Jeremiah's prophetic writings is the promise of the New Covenant in Jeremiah 31:31-34, which Christians believe finds its ultimate fulfillment in Jesus. Unlike the old Mosaic Covenant, which was external and often broken, the New Covenant promised by Jeremiah would be written on the hearts of God's people, signifying a deep and transformative relationship with God.

In the New Testament, Jesus identifies Himself as the mediator of this New Covenant during the Last Supper, establishing that His sacrificial death would bring about the forgiveness of sins and restore the relationship between God and humanity. Through Jesus, the law of God is no longer an external command but is internalized in the hearts of believers, aligning them with God's will and granting them direct access to His presence.

3. The Everlasting King: Jesus' Divine Reign

Jeremiah emphasizes God's sovereignty as the everlasting King over all nations, a theme that Christians believe points directly to Jesus' divine kingship. In the New Testament, Jesus is presented as the King of kings and Lord of lords, whose reign began with His resurrection and will be fully realized at His second coming. Jesus' kingship is not confined to political power but encompasses a spiritual reign that extends over all creation. His divine authority is seen in His ability to conquer sin and death, offering eternal life to those who follow Him.

Jeremiah's depiction of God's kingship over Israel and the nations parallels the New Testament portrayal of Jesus as the divine ruler who will one day return to judge the world and establish His eternal kingdom. Christians believe that Jesus fulfills Jeremiah's vision of a righteous and just King, whose reign brings peace and restoration to the world.

4. Judgment and Redemption: Jesus as the Fulfillment of Jeremiah's Vision

Jeremiah's prophecies often center on the themes of judgment and restoration—God's judgment on His people for their disobedience, followed by the promise of redemption and renewal. Christians see this pattern as foreshadowing the mission of Jesus, who bore the judgment for humanity's sin through His death on the cross and brought redemption through His resurrection.

Just as Jeremiah proclaimed hope and restoration for a broken and exiled people, Christians believe that Jesus offers ultimate hope and restoration for all who are estranged from God. Through His death and resurrection, Jesus fulfills Jeremiah's vision of a restored relationship between God and His people, bringing about a new creation where sin and death no longer reign.

5. Jesus as the Divine Son of God

For Christians, the fulfillment of Jeremiah's prophecies in the life, death, and resurrection of Jesus affirms the divinity of Christ. Jeremiah's writings, which emphasize God's sovereignty, righteousness, and promises of restoration, are seen as pointing forward to the coming of Jesus as the divine Son of God.

This understanding of Jesus' divinity is foundational to Christian faith. Jesus is not merely a prophet or a righteous king; He is the incarnate Word of God, the one through whom all things were made and the one who holds the power to bring about the ultimate redemption of creation. By examining the key passages in Jeremiah and their fulfillment in the New Testament, Christians gain a deeper appreciation for how Jesus is portrayed as both the promised Messiah and the divine ruler, whose reign offers eternal life and salvation to all who believe.

6. Conclusion: The Book of Jeremiah and the Divinity of Christ

The Book of Jeremiah provides profound insight into the nature of God's relationship with His people, emphasizing His justice, mercy, and covenantal faithfulness. For Christians, these themes resonate with the life and mission of Jesus Christ, whose divinity is affirmed through the fulfillment of Jeremiah's messianic prophecies.

From the promise of the Branch of Righteousness to the establishment of the New Covenant, Jeremiah's writings are viewed as prophetic foreshadowings of Jesus, the Divine King who brings about the ultimate redemption and restoration of humanity. Through His death and resurrection, Jesus fulfills the vision of hope that Jeremiah proclaimed, offering a path to salvation and an eternal relationship with God.

In this way, the Book of Jeremiah serves as an important source of messianic prophecy, and its connection to the New Testament deepens the Christian understanding of Jesus as both fully human and fully divine—the Son of God and Savior of the world.

CHAPTER 09

RECAPITULATION OF JESUS' LESSONS IN JEREMIAH

1. Introduction: Jeremiah's Prophecies in Light of Christ

The Book of Jeremiah, written during a time of political upheaval and spiritual decline in the Kingdom of Judah, serves as both a message of divine judgment and a promise of restoration. For Christians, these prophetic writings offer more than historical lessons—they provide profound insights into the life and teachings of Jesus Christ. Jeremiah's prophecies, particularly regarding judgment, repentance, restoration, the New Covenant, and God's kingship, are seen as anticipating and aligning with the key themes in Jesus' own teachings during His earthly ministry.

In this chapter, we will recapitulate how Jesus' lessons are reflected in the Book of Jeremiah, focusing on the major themes of judgment, the call to repentance, the promise of restoration, the New Covenant, and the image of God as King. We will explore how these themes not only echo the message of Jeremiah but are brought to full completion in the person and work of Jesus Christ.

2. Judgment: The Consequences of Sin and Disobedience

Jeremiah's prophecies often center on the theme of judgment, warning Judah of the impending disaster due to their repeated disobedience, idolatry, and social injustice. His ministry was one of unrelenting calls for repentance, warning the people that their rebellion against God would lead to destruction and exile.

Similarly, Jesus' teachings emphasize the reality of divine judgment for sin and the importance of repentance. In many of His parables, Jesus speaks of God's judgment as something inevitable for those who refuse to turn back to Him. Just as Jeremiah warned Judah that their persistent rebellion would lead to destruction, Jesus warned that a failure to repent would lead to eternal separation from God.

2.1 Jesus' Teachings on Judgment

In the New Testament, Jesus frequently addresses the theme of divine judgment, urging His listeners to understand the seriousness of sin and the consequences of living outside of God's will. One of His most striking warnings comes in Luke 13:3:

> "No, I tell you; but unless you repent, you will all likewise perish." (ESV)

This mirrors the calls of Jeremiah, who persistently warned Judah that without repentance, they would face destruction at the hands of foreign powers. In both cases, the heart of the message is clear: judgment is real, and sin has profound consequences, both temporally and eternally.

Jesus, like Jeremiah, speaks of a divine reckoning that awaits those who reject God's grace and continue in their disobedience. Yet, as with Jeremiah, the message of judgment is not devoid of hope—it always carries with it the opportunity for repentance and restoration.

3. Repentance: The Path to Restoration

Jeremiah's mission was not only to announce God's judgment but to call the people of Judah to repentance. Repentance, in the biblical sense, involves turning away from sin and returning to God with a sincere heart. Throughout his ministry, Jeremiah pleaded with the people to recognize their sin, abandon their idolatry, and return to the covenant faithfulness that God desired.

Jesus' teachings on repentance echo this theme. Throughout the Gospels, Jesus calls people to turn from their sinful ways and embrace the kingdom of God. His message was clear: repentance is the gateway to spiritual restoration, the first step toward reconciliation with God.

3.1 Jesus' Call to Repentance

One of the clearest calls to repentance comes from the early stages of Jesus' ministry, in Mark 1:15:

> "The time is fulfilled, and the kingdom of God is at hand; repent and believe in the gospel." (ESV)

Jesus presents repentance as the proper response to the coming of God's kingdom. Like Jeremiah, He calls people to recognize the urgency of their situation—God's judgment is imminent, but through repentance, there is an opportunity for salvation. Jesus' parable of the prodigal son (Luke 15:11-32) also beautifully illustrates the heart of repentance: a realization of sin, a return to the Father, and the experience of grace and forgiveness.

Just as Jeremiah offered Judah a path back to God through repentance, Jesus offers His listeners a way to be restored to right relationship with God through sincere repentance and belief in the good news of salvation.

4. Restoration: Hope Beyond Judgment

Jeremiah's message of judgment was accompanied by a promise of restoration. Even though the people of Judah would face exile, God promised that He would not abandon them forever. He would bring them back from exile and restore them to their land, renewing their covenant relationship. This promise of restoration speaks of God's enduring love and faithfulness, even in the face of human rebellion.

For Christians, this theme of restoration is powerfully fulfilled in Jesus. Jesus not only speaks of individual spiritual restoration but also inaugurates the restoration of all creation. Through His death and resurrection, Jesus opens the way for humanity to be restored to a right relationship with God, and He promises the ultimate restoration of the world when He returns.

4.1 Jesus as the Agent of Restoration

Jesus' miracles and teachings point to His role as the one who brings restoration. In Matthew 11:28, Jesus extends an invitation to those who are weary and burdened:

> "Come to me, all who labor and are heavy laden, and I will give you rest." (ESV)

This invitation echoes the promises of restoration found in Jeremiah. Just as God promised to bring His people back from exile and give them peace, Jesus promises rest, renewal, and healing to those who come to Him in faith. Jesus' ministry of healing, forgiveness, and reconciliation is a foretaste of the ultimate restoration that will be fully realized in His kingdom.

5. The New Covenant: Jesus Fulfills Jeremiah's Prophecy

One of the most significant theological contributions of Jeremiah is the prophecy of the New Covenant, found in Jeremiah 31:31-34. This New Covenant would be different from the Mosaic Covenant; it would involve the internalization of God's law, written on the hearts of the people, and a promise of complete forgiveness of sins.

Christians believe that Jesus' life, death, and resurrection bring this New Covenant into being. During the Last Supper, Jesus explicitly connects His sacrificial death to the New Covenant. In Luke 22:20, He says:

> "This cup that is poured out for you is the new covenant in my blood." (ESV)

Through His death, Jesus establishes a new relationship between God and humanity, one that is based on grace, forgiveness, and the transformation of the heart. No longer would the covenant be based solely on external observance; through the work of the Holy Spirit, believers would experience the law of God written on their hearts, leading to genuine obedience and fellowship with God.

6. The Divine Kingship: Jesus as the Righteous King

Jeremiah presents God as the everlasting King and foretells the coming of a Righteous Branch from the line of David who would reign with justice and righteousness. Christians believe that Jesus fulfills this prophecy, not just as a descendant of David but as the divine King whose reign extends beyond Israel to all nations.

In the New Testament, Jesus is proclaimed as the King of kings and Lord of lords, and His kingship is unlike any earthly rule. Jesus' kingdom is spiritual and eternal, marked by justice, peace, and the ultimate defeat of sin and death.

6.1 Jesus' Kingship in His Teachings

Jesus often spoke of the Kingdom of God, which was at the center of His message. In John 18:36, Jesus clarifies the nature of His kingship:

> "My kingdom is not of this world... My kingdom is not from the world." (ESV)

Unlike the earthly kingdoms that are bound by time, geography, and political power, Jesus' kingdom is eternal and spiritual. It is characterized by righteousness and justice, qualities that reflect the divine kingship described by Jeremiah. Jesus' role as the divine King is fully realized in His resurrection and ascension, and Christians look forward to the day when His reign will be fully established at His second coming.

7. Conclusion: The Continuity of Jeremiah's Message in Jesus' Teachings

The themes found in Jeremiah—judgment, repentance, restoration, the New Covenant, and God's kingship—find their ultimate fulfillment in the person and work of Jesus Christ. For Christians, Jesus not only echoes the prophetic message of Jeremiah but also completes and perfects it. Where Jeremiah offered a vision of future hope and restoration, Jesus brings that hope to reality through His life, death, and resurrection.

Jeremiah's prophecies, which were initially directed toward the people of Judah, resonate throughout the New Testament, offering a deeper understanding of God's plan for humanity. Through Jesus, the lessons of Jeremiah come to life, showing that God's ultimate purpose is not only to judge sin but to restore His people to eternal fellowship with Him. This recapitulation of Jesus' lessons in Jeremiah reminds Christians of the continuity of God's redemptive plan and the profound connection between the Old and New Testaments in revealing the fullness of God's grace and truth.

CHAPTER 10

STUDY DUIDE AND REFLECTION QUESTIONS

This chapter provides a study guide and reflection questions for each chapter of this book on the divinity of Jesus in the Book of Jeremiah. These questions are designed to deepen your understanding of the themes discussed and encourage personal reflection on how these themes connect with the life and work of Jesus Christ. They are suitable for individual study, group discussions, or personal reflection as you explore the prophetic writings of Jeremiah and their fulfillment in Jesus.

Chapter 1: The Historical Context of Jeremiah

Key Themes:

- The political, social, and religious decline of Judah

- Jeremiah's role as a prophet during a time of national crisis

- The impending Babylonian exile and its theological significance

Study Questions:

1. How did the political and social context of Judah during Jeremiah's time influence his message?

2. What were the major religious failures of the people of Judah, and how did these lead to God's judgment?

3. How does understanding the historical context of Jeremiah help to interpret his prophecies?

4. In what ways do you see parallels between the spiritual condition of Judah and the world today?

Reflection Question:

- Jeremiah was known as the "weeping prophet" because of the sorrow he felt for his people. How can we, like Jeremiah, maintain a heart of compassion even while confronting the reality of sin and judgment in our own context?

Chapter 2: The Branch of Righteousness

Key Themes:

- The messianic prophecy of the "Branch of Righteousness" in Jeremiah 23:5-6

- The expectation of a righteous King from the line of David

- Jesus as the fulfillment of this prophecy

Study Questions:

1. What is the significance of the title "Branch of Righteousness" in Jeremiah's prophecy?

2. How does Jeremiah's vision of a righteous King from the line of David foreshadow the coming of Jesus?

3. Why is the phrase "The Lord our righteousness" important in understanding Jesus' divine nature?

4. How does the prophecy of the Branch of Righteousness give hope to the people of Judah in the midst of judgment?

Reflection Question:

- Jesus is called "The Lord our righteousness." In what ways does Jesus' righteousness shape your understanding of what it means to live a holy and just life?

Chapter 3: The New Covenant

Key Themes:

- Jeremiah's prophecy of the New Covenant in Jeremiah 31:31-34

- The limitations of the Mosaic Covenant and the need for a New Covenant

- Jesus as the mediator of the New Covenant through His death and resurrection

Study Questions:

1. What are the key differences between the Old Covenant (Mosaic Covenant) and the New Covenant prophesied by Jeremiah?

2. How does the promise of the New Covenant offer hope for a deeper relationship with God?

3. How does Jesus' life, death, and resurrection fulfill the prophecy of the New Covenant in Jeremiah?

4. What does it mean that the law would be written on the hearts of God's people under the New Covenant?

Reflection Question:

- In what ways do you experience the reality of the New Covenant in your own life, especially in terms of God's law being written on your heart and the promise of forgiveness?

Chapter 4: The Shepherd-King

Key Themes:

- Jeremiah's use of shepherd imagery to critique Israel's leaders

- The failure of the corrupt shepherds (leaders) of Judah

- Jesus as the Good Shepherd who gathers and protects His people

Study Questions:

1. How does Jeremiah use the image of shepherds to describe both good and bad leadership?

2. What were the failures of the leaders (shepherds) in Jeremiah's time, and how did this contribute to Judah's downfall?

3. How is Jesus' role as the Good Shepherd a fulfillment of Jeremiah's vision of righteous leadership?

4. What are some key characteristics of a good shepherd, and how does Jesus embody them?

Reflection Question:

- Jesus describes Himself as the Good Shepherd who lays down His life for the sheep. How does this image of Jesus shape your understanding of His love and care for you personally?

Chapter 5: Suffering, Judgment, and Redemption

Key Themes:

- Jeremiah's prophecies of judgment for sin and the promise of future redemption

- The theme of suffering as a result of sin and rebellion

- Jesus as the one who bears judgment for sin and brings about redemption

Study Questions:

1. Why is the theme of judgment so prominent in Jeremiah's prophecies, and what purpose does it serve in calling the people to repentance?

2. How does Jeremiah balance the message of judgment with the promise of redemption and restoration?

3. How does Jesus take upon Himself the judgment for sin, and how does this fulfill the themes of suffering and redemption in Jeremiah?

4. In what ways does Jesus' death and resurrection offer hope for those facing the consequences of sin?

Reflection Question:

- How does understanding Jesus' role in bearing judgment for your sin affect your view of God's justice and mercy?

Chapter 6: The Divine King

Key Themes:

- Jeremiah's presentation of God as the everlasting King over Israel and the nations

- Jesus as the King of kings and Lord of lords, fulfilling the vision of divine kingship in the Old Testament

- The nature of Jesus' spiritual and universal reign

Study Questions:

1. How does Jeremiah present God as the ultimate King over Israel and the nations?

2. In what ways does the prophecy of a future King in Jeremiah connect to the New Testament descriptions of Jesus as King?

3. How is Jesus' kingship different from earthly kings, and what does it mean that His kingdom is "not of this world" (John 18:36)?

4. What role does Jesus' kingship play in your understanding of His authority in your life today?

Reflection Question:

- Jesus is described as the King who reigns in righteousness and peace. How do you submit to His kingship in your daily life, and what areas of your life are you still struggling to place under His authority?

Chapter 7: Recapitulation of Jesus' Lessons in Jeremiah

Key Themes:

- Jesus' teachings on judgment, repentance, restoration, the New Covenant, and His divine kingship

- The continuity of the messages of Jeremiah and Jesus

- The fulfillment of Jeremiah's prophecies in the person and work of Christ

Study Questions:

1. How do Jesus' teachings on judgment and repentance reflect the message of Jeremiah?

2. In what ways does Jesus bring the restoration promised in Jeremiah to full completion through His life, death, and resurrection?

3. How does Jesus' establishment of the New Covenant fulfill Jeremiah's vision of a transformed relationship with God?

4. What are some of the key lessons from Jeremiah's prophecies that are reflected in Jesus' ministry?

Reflection Question:

- Reflect on the ways in which the themes of judgment, repentance, and restoration in Jeremiah are still relevant to your spiritual journey today. How does Jesus' fulfillment of these themes offer you hope and guidance?

Chapter 8: The Reign of Christ

Key Themes:

- The belief that Jesus' reign began with His resurrection and will be fully realized in His second coming

- The "already" and "not yet" nature of Christ's kingship

- The implications of Jesus' present and future reign for believers

Study Questions:

1. How does the resurrection of Jesus mark the beginning of His reign as King?

2. What does it mean that Jesus' reign is both "already" and "not yet"?

3. How does the anticipation of Jesus' second coming shape the way Christians live in the present?

4. In what ways can believers participate in the mission of Jesus' kingdom while awaiting its full realization?

Reflection Question:

- Jesus' reign is described as both a present reality and a future hope. How does this tension influence the way you live out your faith today? What does it look like to live as a citizen of Christ's kingdom in your everyday life?

Chapter 9: Conclusion: Jeremiah and the Divinity of Christ

Key Themes:

- The prophetic imagery of Jeremiah and its fulfillment in Jesus

- Jesus as the divine fulfillment of the messianic promises in Jeremiah

- The connection between Jeremiah's prophecies and the Christian understanding of Jesus' divinity

Study Questions:

1. How does the Book of Jeremiah contribute to the Christian understanding of Jesus as the divine Messiah?

2. In what ways does Jeremiah's prophecy of the Branch of Righteousness point forward to Jesus' divinity and kingship?

3. How does the establishment of the New Covenant in Jeremiah 31:31-34 enhance our understanding of Jesus' mission and identity?

4. What significance do Jeremiah's prophecies hold for modern Christian faith and theology?

Reflection Question:

- Reflect on the ways in which the Book of Jeremiah has deepened your understanding of Jesus as both divine and messianic. How do these prophetic connections strengthen your faith in Christ's identity and mission?

This study guide and the accompanying reflection questions are meant to facilitate a deeper exploration of the themes discussed throughout the book. By engaging with these questions, you are invited to reflect on the profound connections between Jeremiah's prophetic writings and the person of Jesus Christ, gaining a richer understanding of how the Old Testament points to the New Covenant fulfilled in Christ.

CHAPTER 11

REFLECTION PROMPTS FOR PERSONAL APPLICATION

As you journey through the Book of Jeremiah and its fulfillment in Jesus Christ, it's important not only to grasp the theological and historical significance but also to apply these lessons personally. Reflection and personal application allow you to take the profound truths of Scripture and connect them to your own life, transforming knowledge into action and growth.

This chapter offers reflection prompts that encourage you to examine your relationship with God, your understanding of Jesus' kingship, and your role as a follower of Christ. These prompts are designed to help you internalize the major themes of Jeremiah—judgment, repentance, restoration, the New Covenant, and Jesus' divine kingship—so that they can shape your spiritual journey.

---

1. The Reality of Divine Judgment and Accountability

The theme of judgment is prevalent in Jeremiah, and Jesus continues this theme in His teachings, reminding us that sin has consequences and that we are accountable to God. Reflecting on the reality of divine judgment calls us to examine our lives honestly.

Reflection Prompts:

- Are there areas in your life where you have been ignoring God's commands or willfully disobeying Him? How do you respond when confronted with the reality of sin and judgment?

- How does the concept of divine judgment affect your view of God's holiness and justice? In what ways does this motivate you to live a life of integrity and righteousness?

- Reflect on times when you have felt the weight of guilt or conviction. How did you respond to God's call for repentance, and how did this lead to spiritual growth or healing?

Personal Application:

Spend time in prayer, asking God to reveal areas of your life where you need to repent and seek His forgiveness. Consider making a tangible plan for how you will turn away from sin and pursue a path of obedience to God's will.

---

2. Repentance as a Pathway to Renewal

Repentance is a central theme in both Jeremiah and Jesus' teachings. It is not simply about feeling sorry for sin but about a transformative turning back to God. True repentance leads to spiritual renewal, deeper intimacy with God, and personal restoration.

Reflection Prompts:

- What does repentance mean to you personally? How have you experienced spiritual renewal after times of genuine repentance in your life?

- Are there patterns of sin or unhealthy habits that have been keeping you from a close relationship with God? What steps can you take to break free from these patterns?

- How does God's mercy and willingness to forgive motivate you to seek Him, even when you feel ashamed or distant?

Personal Application:

Take time to reflect on your relationship with God and ask Him to show you areas where repentance is needed. Write a prayer of repentance, acknowledging specific areas of sin, and ask for God's help in making a fresh start.

---

3. Restoration: Finding Hope Beyond Brokenness

Jeremiah's message of restoration gives hope to those who feel broken, abandoned, or far from God. Restoration involves being brought back into right relationship with God and being made whole again through His grace. In Christ, this restoration is made possible for all who believe.

Reflection Prompts:

- Reflect on a time in your life when you felt distant from God. How did He bring about restoration and healing in your life? What role did repentance and faith play in this process?

- In what areas of your life do you currently feel broken, weary, or in need of restoration? How can you invite God into those places of pain or loss?

- How does the promise of future restoration—both personally and for the world—give you hope in the midst of difficult circumstances?

Personal Application:

Consider the areas in your life where you are longing for restoration, whether emotional, spiritual, or relational. Commit these areas to God in prayer, trusting that He can bring healing and renewal. If needed, seek out support from a spiritual mentor, counselor, or trusted friend to help you on this journey of restoration.

---

4. The New Covenant: Experiencing Transformation Through Christ

Jeremiah's prophecy of the New Covenant finds its fulfillment in Jesus, who brings about a new relationship between God and humanity. Under the New Covenant, God's law is written on our hearts, and we are empowered by the Holy Spirit to live in obedience and intimacy with Him.

Reflection Prompts:

- How do you experience the reality of the New Covenant in your own life? In what ways has your heart been transformed by God's grace and His Spirit?

- Reflect on a specific time when you felt the Holy Spirit leading you to make a change, obey God's commands, or act in faith. How did this experience strengthen your relationship with God?

- How does the New Covenant shape your understanding of God's love and forgiveness? What does it mean to live with the law of God written on your heart?

Personal Application:

Spend time reflecting on your life under the New Covenant, thanking God for the gift of His Spirit and the transformation He brings. Journal about the ways you have experienced growth, and ask for continued guidance and strength to live a life that reflects God's will.

---

5. Jesus as the Righteous King: Living Under His Reign

In Jeremiah, the promise of a Righteous King from the line of David points forward to Jesus, whose kingship is eternal and just. Living under the reign of Jesus means submitting to His authority and allowing His values—justice, love, and righteousness—to shape our lives.

Reflection Prompts:

- In what areas of your life have you fully submitted to Jesus' kingship? In what areas do you still struggle to relinquish control or follow His leading?

- How does knowing that Jesus is your King affect the way you make decisions, treat others, and approach difficult situations?

- Reflect on a time when you experienced God's peace and guidance by submitting to Jesus' authority. How did this deepen your trust in Him as your King?

Personal Application:

Take time to examine the areas of your life where you may be holding back from submitting to Jesus' kingship. Write a prayer of surrender, asking Jesus to take full authority over your life and to lead you in His ways.

---

6. Anticipating Christ's Return: Living in Hope

Jeremiah's prophecies look forward to a time of restoration and peace, and Christians believe that this will be fully realized when Jesus returns to establish His kingdom in its fullness. In the meantime, believers are called to live in hope, looking forward to Christ's second coming while faithfully serving Him in the present.

Reflection Prompts:

- How does the promise of Christ's return give you hope in your current life circumstances? In what ways does it help you endure suffering or uncertainty?

- How does your belief in Jesus' second coming affect the way you live each day? Are there areas where you can be more intentional about aligning your life with His kingdom values?

- Reflect on the "already" and "not yet" nature of Christ's kingdom. How do you balance living in the present reality of Jesus' reign while also anticipating His future return?

Personal Application:

Spend time meditating on the promises of Christ's return and the hope of restoration that it brings. Consider how you can live with greater intentionality and purpose, knowing that Jesus is coming again. Set a goal to serve others or share the hope of Christ with someone who may be struggling.

---

7. Conclusion: Integrating Jeremiah's Message into Your Spiritual Journey

Jeremiah's prophetic message offers a powerful reflection on God's justice, mercy, and promises of restoration, all of which are fulfilled in Jesus Christ. By applying the themes of judgment, repentance, restoration, and divine kingship to your personal spiritual journey, you can deepen your understanding of God's plan for your life and grow in your relationship with Him.

Reflection Prompts:

- How has your understanding of God's justice and mercy been shaped by Jeremiah's prophecies and Jesus' fulfillment of them?

- What areas of your life have been most affected by studying these themes, and how can you continue to grow in your relationship with God?

- How can you use the lessons from Jeremiah to encourage others who are struggling with sin, brokenness, or a sense of distance from God?

Personal Application:

Take some time to reflect on your journey through the Book of Jeremiah and the life of Jesus. Write down key takeaways that have impacted you, and make a plan for how you will continue to apply these lessons in your daily walk with Christ.

These reflection prompts are designed to help you internalize the lessons from Jeremiah and see their fulfillment in Jesus. By engaging with these themes on a personal level, you can grow in your understanding of God's character, deepen your faith, and experience transformation through the Holy Spirit. Let this reflection be a starting point for continual growth and discipleship in your journey with Christ.

CHAPTER 12

GROUP DISCUSSION TOPICS

The study of Jeremiah and its connection to the divinity of Jesus provides rich material for group discussions. Exploring these themes in a group setting allows for a deeper understanding of biblical texts, shared insights, and practical applications in everyday life. The following group discussion topics are designed to facilitate engaging conversations and encourage participants to reflect on how the themes from Jeremiah and their fulfillment in Jesus impact their faith, actions, and community.

Each discussion topic is based on a specific theme from the chapters of this study, with suggested questions to guide the conversation. These topics are ideal for Bible study groups, small groups, or church classes.

---

1. Judgment and Repentance: Responding to God's Call

Overview: Both Jeremiah and Jesus call people to repentance in light of God's judgment on sin. This topic encourages a discussion on the role of judgment in our faith and how repentance leads to restoration.

Discussion Questions:

- How do you view God's judgment? Do you see it as an act of justice, mercy, or both? Why?

- Why do you think it's difficult for people to respond to calls for repentance, both in Jeremiah's time and today?

- Can you share a time when you felt God calling you to repentance? How did you respond, and what was the outcome?

- What role does repentance play in our daily spiritual walk? How can we encourage each other to embrace repentance as a pathway to growth and healing?

Discussion Challenge:

- Consider how your group can foster a culture of repentance and accountability within your church or community. Discuss practical ways to create an environment where people feel safe to confess, repent, and seek restoration.

---

2. The New Covenant: Understanding Our Relationship with God

Overview: Jeremiah's prophecy of the New Covenant points forward to the relationship Christians have with God through Jesus. This discussion will explore the nature of the New Covenant and how it changes the way we relate to God.

Discussion Questions:

- How is the New Covenant different from the Old Covenant, and why is this difference important?

- What does it mean for God's law to be written on our hearts? How do we experience this internal transformation today?

- How does the New Covenant affect our understanding of forgiveness and grace?

- In what ways can we live more fully in the reality of the New Covenant? How can we rely on the Holy Spirit to guide us in our relationship with God?

Discussion Challenge:

- As a group, discuss ways in which you can collectively live out the New Covenant in your community. How can you embody the values of forgiveness, grace, and love in your relationships with others?

---

3. The Shepherd-King: Jesus' Leadership and Our Role as Followers

Overview: In both Jeremiah and the New Testament, the image of a shepherd is used to describe leadership. Jesus as the Good Shepherd offers a model of servant leadership that we are called to follow.

Discussion Questions:

- What are the characteristics of a good shepherd, as described in Jeremiah and Jesus' teachings? How does Jesus model these characteristics in His life and ministry?

- How do we distinguish between good and bad leadership in our churches, communities, and even within ourselves?

- Jesus laid down His life for His sheep. How does His example challenge us to serve and care for others sacrificially?

- What does it mean to be a faithful follower of the Good Shepherd? How do we listen to His voice and follow His guidance in our daily lives?

Discussion Challenge:

- Discuss how your group can serve as shepherds to your community. Identify specific ways to care for those who are vulnerable, lost, or in need of spiritual guidance, and make a plan to engage in acts of service.

---

4. Restoration and Hope: Finding Redemption in God's Plan

Overview: Jeremiah speaks of judgment but also offers the promise of restoration. This discussion focuses on God's promise of restoration, how it applies to us today, and how we can be agents of restoration in a broken world.

Discussion Questions:

- How does the promise of restoration in Jeremiah give hope to people facing difficult circumstances, both in his time and in ours?

- In what areas of your life do you currently need restoration? How can you lean on God for healing and renewal?

- How does Jesus' role in bringing ultimate restoration through His death and resurrection shape your faith and hope?

- What practical ways can we be agents of God's restoration in our communities—bringing healing, reconciliation, and renewal to those around us?

Discussion Challenge:

- As a group, brainstorm ways to bring hope and restoration to people in need—whether through prayer, acts of kindness, community service, or support for those going through difficult times. Plan a specific project to bring restoration to your community.

---

5. The Reign of Christ: Living in the Kingdom of God

Overview: The reign of Christ began with His resurrection and will be fully realized at His second coming. This discussion will explore how we live in the "already" and "not yet" of Christ's kingdom and what it means to live under Jesus' reign today.

Discussion Questions:

- How do you understand the concept of the "already" and "not yet" of Christ's reign? How does this tension influence the way we live our faith?

- In what ways do we experience Christ's reign in our everyday lives? How does His kingship impact the way we make decisions and live according to kingdom values?

- How can we cultivate a kingdom mindset in our daily interactions with others? What does it mean to live with Christ as King in our relationships, work, and community involvement?

- What hope does the promise of Christ's return bring to you personally? How can we live with that hope while remaining focused on serving Christ in the present?

Discussion Challenge:

- Challenge your group to adopt a "kingdom mindset" for the coming week. Discuss specific ways to live out kingdom values, such as justice, mercy, and love, in your homes, workplaces, and communities. Share your experiences in the next meeting.

---

6. Jesus as the Divine King: Submitting to His Authority

Overview: Jeremiah presents God as the ultimate King, and Christians believe that Jesus fulfills this role as the divine King. This discussion will focus on what it means to submit to Jesus' authority and live under His kingship.

Discussion Questions:

- What does it mean to acknowledge Jesus as King in your life? In what ways do we struggle with submitting to His authority?

- How does living under the kingship of Jesus challenge our cultural values, especially around autonomy, power, and success?

- Reflect on a time when you fully trusted in Jesus' leadership in your life. How did that experience shape your understanding of His kingship?

- In what areas of your life do you need to surrender to Jesus' authority? How can the group support you in this journey?

Discussion Challenge:

- As a group, commit to spending time in prayer, asking for guidance on how to surrender more fully to Jesus' kingship. Encourage each other to identify one area of life where they need to trust in Jesus' authority and share how they are actively making that change.

---

7. The New Covenant: Embracing Transformation Through Jesus

Overview: The New Covenant is central to the message of Jeremiah and is fulfilled in Jesus. This discussion focuses on how we experience transformation through the New Covenant and how this impacts our lives as believers.

Discussion Questions:

- How does the New Covenant change the way we relate to God compared to the Old Covenant? How does the internal transformation promised in the New Covenant affect your relationship with God?

- In what ways do you experience God's law being written on your heart? How does the Holy Spirit guide and transform you in your daily walk?

- How does the New Covenant offer hope for forgiveness, grace, and personal transformation? What does it look like to live out that hope in practical ways?

- How can we support each other in experiencing and embracing the transformation that comes through Jesus and the New Covenant?

Discussion Challenge:

- Discuss how your group can encourage one another in their spiritual transformation under the New Covenant. Share personal testimonies of how God has been working in your life recently and how the group can help you continue growing in faith.

These group discussion topics are designed to promote meaningful conversations about the themes of Jeremiah and their fulfillment in Jesus Christ. By engaging with these topics in a group setting, participants can grow together in understanding, faith, and application of biblical truths. Encourage openness, active listening, and a spirit of prayer as your group journeys through these important discussions.

APPENDICES A

LIST OF MESSIANIC PSALMS

The Psalms, a collection of poetic hymns and prayers, are rich with messianic prophecies—verses that Christians believe foreshadow the coming of Jesus Christ, the Messiah. These psalms reflect themes of the Messiah's kingship, suffering, victory, and ultimate reign. While some of these psalms have an immediate context related to the life of David or other historical events, Christians view many of them as pointing forward to Jesus and His work of salvation.

Below is a list of key Messianic Psalms and their significance within the context of Jesus' life, ministry, death, and resurrection:

Psalm 2: The Reign of the Lord's Anointed

Key Verses:

- Psalm 2:7 – "The Lord said to me, 'You are my Son; today I have begotten you.'"

- Psalm 2:12 – "Kiss the Son, lest he be angry, and you perish in the way, for his wrath is quickly kindled. Blessed are all who take refuge in him."

Messianic Significance: This psalm presents the Messiah as God's anointed King, who will reign over all the nations. The declaration of the Sonship of the Messiah in verse 7 is echoed in the New Testament, particularly in the baptism of Jesus (Matthew 3:17) and the Transfiguration (Mark 9:7), where God proclaims Jesus as His beloved Son.

Psalm 16: The Holy One Who Does Not See Decay

Key Verses:

- Psalm 16:10 – "For you will not abandon my soul to Sheol, or let your holy one see corruption."

Messianic Significance: This psalm expresses trust in God's deliverance and the hope of resurrection. In Acts 2:25-31, Peter directly applies this psalm to Jesus, explaining that while David died and was buried, Jesus was raised from the dead, fulfilling the promise that the Holy One would not see decay.

Psalm 22: The Suffering Messiah

Key Verses:

- Psalm 22:1 – "My God, my God, why have you forsaken me?"

- Psalm 22:16 – "For dogs encompass me; a company of evildoers encircles me; they have pierced my hands and feet."

- Psalm 22:18 – "They divide my garments among them, and for my clothing they cast lots."

Messianic Significance: Psalm 22 is perhaps the most well-known messianic psalm related to the suffering of Jesus. Jesus Himself quotes verse 1 on the cross (Matthew 27:46), expressing His sense of abandonment. The psalm's vivid description of crucifixion-like suffering, including the piercing of hands and feet and the casting of lots for clothing, is seen as a prophetic foreshadowing of Jesus' crucifixion.

Psalm 23: The Good Shepherd

Key Verses:

- Psalm 23:1 – "The Lord is my shepherd; I shall not want."

Messianic Significance: While traditionally seen as a psalm of comfort and trust in God's provision, Christians also see Jesus as the fulfillment of the Good Shepherd described in Psalm 23. In John 10, Jesus declares Himself as the Good Shepherd who lays down His life for the sheep, echoing the themes of provision, protection, and guidance found in this psalm.

Psalm 24: The King of Glory

Key Verses:

- Psalm 24:7-8 – "Lift up your heads, O gates! And be lifted up, O ancient doors, that the King of glory may come in. Who is this King of glory? The Lord, strong and mighty, the Lord, mighty in battle!"

Messianic Significance: This psalm celebrates the coming of the Lord as the King of glory, victorious in battle and reigning in majesty. For Christians, Jesus is the King of glory who triumphantly entered Jerusalem before His crucifixion (Palm Sunday) and will return again in glory to reign eternally.

Psalm 40: The Obedient Servant

Key Verses:

- Psalm 40:6-8 – "In sacrifice and offering you have not delighted, but you have given me an open ear. Burnt offering and sin offering you have not required. Then I said,

'Behold, I have come; in the scroll of the book it is written of me: I delight to do your will, O my God; your law is within my heart.'"

Messianic Significance: This psalm expresses the Messiah's obedience to God's will. In Hebrews 10:5-10, the writer quotes this psalm and applies it to Jesus, showing that Jesus' ultimate obedience to the Father's will—through His death on the cross—fulfilled God's plan of salvation.

Psalm 45: The Eternal Throne of the Messiah
Key Verses:

- Psalm 45:6-7 – "Your throne, O God, is forever and ever. The scepter of your kingdom is a scepter of uprightness; you have loved righteousness and hated wickedness."

Messianic Significance: Psalm 45 speaks of the eternal reign of the Messiah as a righteous King. This passage is applied to Jesus in Hebrews 1:8-9, affirming His divinity and eternal kingship. The description of the Messiah's throne as "forever and ever" aligns with the Christian belief in Jesus' eternal reign as King of kings.

Psalm 69: The Zealous and Suffering Messiah
Key Verses:

- Psalm 69:9 – "For zeal for your house has consumed me, and the reproaches of those who reproach you have fallen on me."

- Psalm 69:21 – "They gave me poison for food, and for my thirst they gave me sour wine to drink."

Messianic Significance: This psalm describes the suffering and reproach faced by the righteous servant of God. In the New Testament, verse 9 is quoted in John 2:17 when Jesus cleanses the temple, showing His zeal for God's house. Verse 21 is seen as a direct prophecy of the crucifixion, as Jesus was offered sour wine to drink while on the cross (Matthew 27:48).

Psalm 72: The Reign of the Messiah

Key Verses:

- Psalm 72:8 – "May he have dominion from sea to sea, and from the River to the ends of the earth!"

- Psalm 72:17 – "May his name endure forever, his fame continue as long as the sun! May people be blessed in him, all nations call him blessed!"

Messianic Significance: Psalm 72 describes the ideal reign of a righteous king who rules with justice and brings blessing to all nations. Christians interpret this psalm as pointing to Jesus, whose kingdom is universal and whose reign brings blessing to all peoples (Philippians 2:9-11).

Psalm 89: The Covenant with David

Key Verses:

- Psalm 89:3-4 – "You have said, 'I have made a covenant with my chosen one; I have sworn to David my servant: I will establish your offspring forever, and build your throne for all generations.'"

- Psalm 89:27 – "And I will make him the firstborn, the highest of the kings of the earth."

Messianic Significance: This psalm reflects God's covenant with David, promising that his descendants would reign forever. For Christians, this promise is fulfilled in Jesus, who is the eternal King from the line of David, as affirmed in Luke 1:32-33, where the angel tells Mary that her son Jesus will sit on the throne of His father David forever.

Psalm 110: The Priestly Messiah

Key Verses:

- Psalm 110:1 – "The Lord says to my Lord: 'Sit at my right hand, until I make your enemies your footstool.'"

- Psalm 110:4 – "The Lord has sworn and will not change his mind, 'You are a priest forever after the order of Melchizedek.'"

Messianic Significance: Psalm 110 is one of the most frequently quoted psalms in the New Testament. Verse 1 is cited in Matthew 22:44, where Jesus uses it to explain His divine authority. Verse 4 is significant because it presents the Messiah as both King and eternal High Priest, a role Christians believe Jesus fulfills through His death, resurrection, and ascension.

Psalm 118: The Rejected Stone

Key Verses:

- Psalm 118:22-23 – "The stone that the builders rejected has become the cornerstone. This is the Lord's doing; it is marvelous in our eyes."

- Psalm 118:26 – "Blessed is he who comes in the name of the Lord!"

Messianic Significance: Jesus applies verse 22 to Himself in Matthew 21:42, indicating that He is the "rejected stone" who becomes the cornerstone of God's work of salvation. The cry of "Blessed is he who comes in the name of the Lord!" was also shouted by the crowds during Jesus' triumphal entry into Jerusalem (Matthew 21:9).

These Messianic Psalms are integral to understanding how the Old Testament points forward to Jesus. They highlight key aspects of His identity, mission, and reign, offering a prophetic glimpse of the Messiah who would bring salvation to the world. Through these psalms, believers can see the continuity of God's redemptive plan from the time of David to its fulfillment in Christ.

Just as the prospectors were beginning to settle into their new way of life, nature unleashed its fury upon the boomtown with a vengeance. A dark and ominous storm cloud, pregnant with rain, loomed on the horizon, and the wind whispered foreboding tales of what was to come.

CROSS REFERENCES TO NEW TESTAMENT

Appendices: Cross-References to New Testament Fulfillments of Messianic Psalms

The Messianic Psalms in the Old Testament contain prophecies and imagery that Christians believe are fulfilled in the life, death, resurrection, and reign of Jesus Christ. These cross-references between the Psalms and the New Testament show the direct fulfillment of these ancient prophecies in Jesus' life and ministry. Below is a list of key Messianic Psalms with their corresponding New Testament fulfillments.

Psalm 2: The Reign of the Lord's Anointed

Psalm 2:7:

> "The Lord said to me, 'You are my Son; today I have begotten you.'"

New Testament Fulfillment:

- Matthew 3:17: "And behold, a voice from heaven said, 'This is my beloved Son, with whom I am well pleased.'"

- Acts 13:33: "This he has fulfilled to us their children by raising Jesus, as also it is written in the second Psalm, 'You are my Son, today I have begotten you.'"

Psalm 2:12:

> "Kiss the Son, lest he be angry, and you perish in the way..."

New Testament Fulfillment:

- Revelation 6:16-17: "...hide us from the face of him who is seated on the throne, and from the wrath of the Lamb, for the great day of their wrath has come, and who can stand?"

Psalm 16: The Holy One Who Does Not See Decay

Psalm 16:10:

> "For you will not abandon my soul to Sheol, or let your holy one see corruption."

New Testament Fulfillment:

- Acts 2:31: "He foresaw and spoke about the resurrection of the Christ, that he was not abandoned to Hades, nor did his flesh see corruption."

- Acts 13:35: "Therefore he says also in another psalm, 'You will not let your Holy One see corruption.'"

Psalm 22: The Suffering Messiah

Psalm 22:1:

> "My God, my God, why have you forsaken me?"

New Testament Fulfillment:

- Matthew 27:46: "And about the ninth hour Jesus cried out with a loud voice, saying, 'Eli, Eli, lema sabachthani?' that is, 'My God, my God, why have you forsaken me?'"

Psalm 22:16:

> "For dogs encompass me; a company of evildoers encircles me; they have pierced my hands and feet."

New Testament Fulfillment:

- John 20:25: "Unless I see in his hands the mark of the nails, and place my finger into the mark of the nails, and place my hand into his side, I will never believe."

Psalm 22:18:

> "They divide my garments among them, and for my clothing they cast lots."

New Testament Fulfillment:

- Matthew 27:35: "And when they had crucified him, they divided his garments among them by casting lots."

Psalm 23: The Good Shepherd

Psalm 23:1:

> "The Lord is my shepherd; I shall not want."

New Testament Fulfillment:

- John 10:11: "I am the good shepherd. The good shepherd lays down his life for the sheep."

- Hebrews 13:20: "Now may the God of peace who brought again from the dead our Lord Jesus, the great shepherd of the sheep..."

Psalm 24: The King of Glory

Psalm 24:7-10:

> "Lift up your heads, O gates! And be lifted up, O ancient doors, that the King of glory may come in. Who is this King of glory? The Lord, strong and mighty..."

New Testament Fulfillment:

- 1 Corinthians 2:8: "...none of the rulers of this age understood this, for if they had, they would not have crucified the Lord of glory."

- Revelation 19:16: "On his robe and on his thigh he has a name written, King of kings and Lord of lords."

Psalm 40: The Obedient Servant

Psalm 40:6-8:

> "In sacrifice and offering you have not delighted, but you have given me an open ear... I delight to do your will, O my God; your law is within my heart."

New Testament Fulfillment:

- Hebrews 10:5-7: "Consequently, when Christ came into the world, he said, 'Sacrifices and offerings you have not desired, but a body have you prepared for me... Behold, I have come to do your will, O God.'"

Psalm 45: The Eternal Throne of the Messiah

Psalm 45:6-7:

> "Your throne, O God, is forever and ever. The scepter of your kingdom is a scepter of uprightness; you have loved righteousness and hated wickedness."

New Testament Fulfillment:

- Hebrews 1:8-9: "But of the Son he says, 'Your throne, O God, is forever and ever, the scepter of uprightness is the scepter of your kingdom.'"

Psalm 69: The Zealous and Suffering Messiah

Psalm 69:9:

> "For zeal for your house has consumed me, and the reproaches of those who reproach you have fallen on me."

New Testament Fulfillment:

- John 2:17: "His disciples remembered that it was written, 'Zeal for your house will consume me.'"

Psalm 69:21:

> "They gave me poison for food, and for my thirst they gave me sour wine to drink."

New Testament Fulfillment:

- Matthew 27:48: "And one of them at once ran and took a sponge, filled it with sour wine, and put it on a reed and gave it to him to drink."

Psalm 72: The Reign of the Messiah

Psalm 72:8:

> "May he have dominion from sea to sea, and from the River to the ends of the earth!"

New Testament Fulfillment:

- Philippians 2:9-10: "Therefore God has highly exalted him and bestowed on him the name that is above every name, so that at the name of Jesus every knee should bow, in heaven and on earth and under the earth."

Psalm 89: The Covenant with David

Psalm 89:3-4:

> "I have made a covenant with my chosen one; I have sworn to David my servant: I will establish your offspring forever, and build your throne for all generations."

New Testament Fulfillment:

- Luke 1:32-33: "He will be great and will be called the Son of the Most High. And the Lord God will give to him the throne of his father David, and he will reign over the house of Jacob forever, and of his kingdom there will be no end."

Psalm 110: The Priestly Messiah

Psalm 110:1:

> "The Lord says to my Lord: 'Sit at my right hand, until I make your enemies your footstool.'"

New Testament Fulfillment:

- Matthew 22:44: "The Lord said to my Lord, 'Sit at my right hand, until I put your enemies under your feet.'"

- Acts 2:34-35: "For David did not ascend into the heavens, but he himself says, 'The Lord said to my Lord, Sit at my right hand, until I make your enemies your footstool.'"

Psalm 110:4:

> "You are a priest forever after the order of Melchizedek."

New Testament Fulfillment:

- Hebrews 7:17: "For it is witnessed of him, 'You are a priest forever, after the order of Melchizedek.'"

Psalm 118: The Rejected Stone

Psalm 118:22-23:

> "The stone that the builders rejected has become the cornerstone. This is the Lord's doing; it is marvelous in our eyes."

New Testament Fulfillment:

- Matthew 21:42: "Jesus said to them, 'Have you never read in the Scriptures: The stone that the builders rejected has become the cornerstone; this was the Lord's doing, and it is marvelous in our eyes?'"

Psalm 118:26:

> "Blessed is he who comes in the name of the Lord!"

New Testament Fulfillment:

- Matthew 21:9: "And the crowds that went before him and that followed him were shouting, 'Hosanna to the Son of David! Blessed is he who comes in the name of the Lord! Hosanna in the highest!'"

Conclusion

The cross-references between the Messianic Psalms and their New Testament fulfillments illustrate the continuity of God's redemptive plan. These Psalms not only reflect Israel's hope for a coming Messiah but also find their complete fulfillment in the life, ministry, and work of Jesus Christ. The New Testament writers frequently pointed to these Psalms as evidence of Jesus' identity as the long-awaited Messiah, King, and Savior. Through these connections, Christians gain a fuller understanding of how the Old and New Testaments together reveal the unfolding of God's salvation history.

APPENDICES C

ADDITIONAL RESOURCES FOR FURTHER STUDY

For those interested in exploring the themes of Jeremiah, Messianic prophecy, and the fulfillment of Old Testament prophecies in the life of Jesus, there are numerous resources available to deepen your understanding. Below is a list of recommended books, commentaries, websites, and tools to further your study of these rich biblical themes.

Books

1. Brown, Michael L. Answering Jewish Objections to Jesus (Baker Books, 2000)

- This book provides detailed responses to common objections to Jesus' Messiahship, specifically addressing the fulfillment of Messianic prophecies in the Old Testament.

2. Kaiser, Walter C. The Messiah in the Old Testament (Zondervan, 1995)

- A scholarly exploration of the Messianic prophecies throughout the Old Testament, focusing on how they point to Jesus. Kaiser's work is particularly helpful for understanding the Messianic connections in books like Jeremiah, Isaiah, and Psalms.

3. Wright, N.T. Jesus and the Victory of God (Fortress Press, 1996)

- A thorough examination of the life and mission of Jesus from a historical and theological perspective. Wright connects Old Testament expectations of the Messiah with the reality of Jesus' ministry.

4. France, R.T. Jesus and the Old Testament (Regent College Publishing, 1997)

- This book provides a comprehensive analysis of how Jesus understood and fulfilled the Old Testament prophecies, including those found in the Psalms and Prophets.

5. Hamilton, Victor P. Handbook on the Pentateuch: Genesis, Exodus, Leviticus, Numbers, Deuteronomy (Baker Academic, 2005)

- While focused on the Pentateuch, this handbook provides excellent insight into the covenantal themes that are later expanded upon in Jeremiah and fulfilled in the New Testament.

6. Brueggemann, Walter. A Commentary on Jeremiah: Exile and Homecoming (Eerdmans, 1998)

- This commentary focuses on the themes of judgment, exile, and restoration in Jeremiah, providing a comprehensive theological analysis of the book's message and its prophetic significance.

Study Bibles

1. The Ryrie Study Bible: Expanded Edition (Moody Publishers, 1994)

- This study Bible offers helpful notes on the Messianic prophecies in Jeremiah and the Psalms, with cross-references to the New Testament to show how these were fulfilled in Christ.

2. The ESV Study Bible (Crossway, 2008)

- The ESV Study Bible includes extensive notes on the Old Testament prophecies, including those in Jeremiah, as well as articles that explore the connections between the Old and New Testaments.

Commentaries

1. Thompson, J.A. The Book of Jeremiah (The New International Commentary on the Old Testament, Eerdmans, 1980)

- A detailed and scholarly commentary on the Book of Jeremiah, exploring its historical context, theological themes, and its Messianic prophecies.

2. Kidner, Derek. Psalms 1–72 and Psalms 73–150 (The Tyndale Old Testament Commentaries, IVP Academic, 1973)

- Kidner's commentary on the Psalms offers valuable insight into the Messianic themes within the Psalms and how they relate to the New Testament's interpretation of these texts.

3. Keener, Craig S. The IVP Bible Background Commentary: New Testament (IVP Academic, 1994)

- This commentary provides historical and cultural context for the New Testament's references to Old Testament prophecies, including those from the Psalms and Jeremiah.

Online Resources and Websites

1. Bible Gateway (https://www.biblegateway.com/)

- A searchable online Bible resource with various translations and commentaries. The site includes cross-references, study notes, and commentaries that help trace Messianic themes from the Old Testament to the New.

2. Blue Letter Bible (https://www.blueletterbible.org/)

- An excellent tool for word studies, cross-referencing, and accessing Strong's Concordance. It is particularly useful for exploring Messianic prophecies and their fulfillment in the New Testament.

3. The Bible Project (https://bibleproject.com/)

- Offers animated videos, podcasts, and articles that explore biblical themes, including prophetic literature and how Old Testament prophecies, like those in Jeremiah, point to Jesus.

4. Got Questions Ministries (https://www.gotquestions.org/)

- A website offering thousands of articles on theological topics, including in-depth answers to questions about Messianic prophecies, Jeremiah's role as a prophet, and Jesus' fulfillment of these prophecies.

5. Monergism (https://www.monergism.com/)

- Provides a wide range of articles, sermons, and book recommendations on topics like the Messianic Psalms, prophetic literature, and Jesus' fulfillment of Old Testament prophecies.

Academic Journals and Articles

1. Journal for the Study of the Old Testament

- A leading academic journal that frequently publishes articles on Old Testament prophecy, including Messianic themes in Jeremiah and the Psalms.

2. Journal of Biblical Literature

- A scholarly journal that includes in-depth studies on biblical texts, often focusing on the connections between Old Testament prophecies and their New Testament fulfillment.

3. Biblica

- Offers free access to biblical studies, including scholarly articles on the prophetic books of the Old Testament and the interpretation of Messianic prophecies.

Bible Concordances and Dictionaries

1. Strong's Exhaustive Concordance of the Bible

- This classic tool is invaluable for in-depth word studies, especially for tracing the Hebrew terms used in the

Messianic prophecies of Jeremiah and the Psalms. Available in both physical format and online via Blue Letter Bible.

2. Vine's Complete Expository Dictionary of Old and New Testament Words (Thomas Nelson, 1996)

- A helpful resource for studying the original Hebrew and Greek words used in the Messianic prophecies, providing a deeper understanding of key terms related to the Messiah.

3. The New Bible Dictionary (InterVarsity Press, 1996)

- This comprehensive dictionary includes entries on the Messianic prophecies, Old Testament prophets, and key theological themes relevant to Jeremiah and the Psalms.

Study Tools and Devotionals

1. John Piper's Look at the Book Series (Desiring God)

- This free online video series features detailed, verse-by-verse studies of various Bible passages, including Messianic texts. Piper's teaching highlights the connections between Old Testament prophecies and their fulfillment in Jesus.

2. Tim Keller's Sermons (Gospel in Life)

- Tim Keller's sermons often focus on how Jesus fulfills Old Testament prophecy. His engaging style brings out the practical applications of Messianic themes, making it easier to apply them to daily life.

3. Charles Spurgeon's Treasury of David

- This classic commentary on the Psalms offers devotional insights into the Messianic Psalms and their spiritual significance. Spurgeon's reflections can provide both theological depth and personal inspiration.

These additional resources offer valuable insights for anyone looking to further explore the connections between the Old Testament and New Testament, particularly how the Book of Jeremiah and the Psalms point forward to Jesus. Whether you are a student, teacher, or lifelong learner, these books, websites, and tools can help deepen your study and reflection on these profound biblical themes.